* *

"In this volume, replete with spiritual wisdom, Paul Higginson invites us to undertake a pilgrimage into the religious imagination. He identifies a serious problem at the heart of contemporary Christian identity: its inability to 'read the signs of the times', to borrow a phrase from Vatican II.

Doing Christianity is an invitation to rediscover for our time the importance of what Richard Rohr (OFM) describes as 'lifestyle Christianity', probably the earliest form of Christianity known to those first century Jewish-Christians who sought to emulate in their lives Jesus' ministry, founded upon *kingdom values*: 'God's Kingdom is close at hand; repent, and believe the good news' (Mark 1:15).

In this regard, Higginson draws our attention to the important distinction between *orthodoxy (right beliefs about Jesus)* and *orthopraxis (right living in imitation of Jesus)*, reflecting a too often neglected verse in the Letter of James: 'If good works do not accompany faith, it is dead' (2:17). It is no accident that of the teaching attributed to Jesus in the New Testament, about 75% of it (directly or indirectly) has to do with compassion/forgiveness, a theme at the heart of this simple and affecting book, one that brings to life the living faith of Jesus in the power of the Spirit."

PETER W. KEENAN
Author of *The Birth of Jesus the Jew: Midrash and the Infancy Gospels*,
and *The Death of Jesus the Jew: Midrash in the Shadow of the Holocaust*

* * *

* * *

"Paul Higginson asks us to walk with, and listen to, Jesus of Nazareth as we make an interior pilgrimage, using this book as our guide. *Doing Christianity* shows us how to experience that infectious 'Joy of the Gospel' which enables us to accept ourselves as we are, acknowledging that we are a pilgrim people, united in living 'the joys and the hopes, the griefs and the anxieties of this age' (Gaudium et Spes 1), but always assured that we walk in the company of the Risen Lord."

FR SHAUN MIDDLETON
Priest and Psychotherapist

* * *

Doing Christianity

How religion is about
what you do, not what you believe

PAUL HIGGINSON

columba
BOOKS

First published in 2023 by

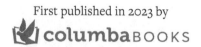 columbaBOOKS

Block 3b, Bracken Business Park,
Bracken Road, Sandyford,Dublin 18, D18 K277
www.columbabooks.com

ISBN: 978-1-78218-397-6

Set in Freight Text Pro and Freight Sans Pro 11.5/15.5
Cover and book design by Alba Esteban | Alestura Design

Frontcover image:
Watercolour illustration © 'The Road to Emmaus'
by Thomas Plunkett PPRWS.

Printed by SprintPrint, Ireland.

ABOUT THE AUTHOR

PAUL HIGGINSON taught Religious Education and Politics for over 35 years and was Assistant Principal at St Dominic's Sixth Form College in Harrow. He has a postgraduate diploma in Social Ethics, specialising in Catholic Social Teaching. Before he began teaching, he worked in a halfway house for people diagnosed with schizophrenia and later spent time working with St Mother Teresa's Missionaries of Charity in Calcutta. He is now an Inspector with the Catholic Schools Inspectorate in England and a volunteer speaker for the charity Mary's Meals. Married with three children he lives in Bushey, Hertfordshire.

Contents

ACKNOWLEDGEMENTS – 9

INTRODUCTION – 11

STARTING OUT - *A PILGRIMAGE WITHIN* – 13

STEP ONE - *WHO IS GOD?* – 24

STEP TWO - *WHO IS JESUS?* – 61

STEP THREE - *WHO AM I?* – 108

STEP FOUR - *A NEW WAY OF SEEING* – 144

STEP FIVE - *A NEW WAY OF DOING* – 189

STEP SIX - *A NEW WAY OF GIVING* – 218

STEP SEVEN - *A NEW WAY OF PRAYING* – 240

STEP EIGHT - *A NEW WAY OF RECEIVING* – 276

STEP NINE - *COMING HOME* – 298

Acknowledgements

To my wife Sue, for her constant loving support, and for reading the early drafts and suggesting improvements. To my children Katie, Anna and David, for their encouragement. To my friend Peter Keenan for his wise advice and insightful suggestions. To Sister Janet Fearns FMDM who first asked me to write about the Gospel and who has encouraged me ever since. To Fr Jim McNicholas for his inspiring homilies, and to the parishioners past and present of the Sacred Heart Church in Bushey. To Thomas Plunkett for his beautiful front cover painting of the Road to Emmaus. To Garry and the team at Columba Books who took this project on and brought it to fruition. And finally, to the staff and students at St Dominic's Sixth Form College in Harrow, where I taught for thirty-four years, for constantly showing me what 'Doing Christianity' looks like.

Introduction

*I wish not merely to be called Christian, but
also to be Christian.*
- St Ignatius

For many years the churches have taught that believing in XYZ makes you a Christian; assenting to certain doctrines and dogmas qualifies for 'club membership' (and if you have incorrect beliefs you may be in big trouble). The theologian Marcus Borg put it like this, 'I thought that the Christian life was about believing in a variety of things that didn't make a lot of sense, but (I thought) that's what faith was all about'.

A faith that relies on thinking the right things (and coming up with complex ways to defend such thoughts) soon crumbles when life intervenes and throws doubts our way. Hence the steady drift away from organised Christianity in western countries, especially among young people. The demographics suggest that within a generation, traditional church-going Christianity in the West will disappear entirely, unless something changes. Sterile theological debates have had their day: 99% of people no longer pay any attention to them. An excessive emphasis on beliefs, 'correct thinking', will only get us so far.

The gospel writers tell us that Jesus was less worried about instilling in his disciples a system of beliefs and more concerned with changing their behaviour. He spoke in parables not theological jargon. What concerns Jesus is how we act rather than the ideas we hold; he calls us to be people who forgive, he urges us to be generous and compassion-ate with others, and to pursue social justice and the way of peace. There is a 'bias towards action' in the gospel. Jesus tells us that if you don't do it, then you don't believe it; if you don't do it then you haven't heard it or seen it. It's only when we start to actually 'do Christianity' that we can truly believe, in our hearts, what we say we believe all along in our heads.

Christianity is a way of living, not a way of believing. Of course, beliefs serve a function (and you will find many of my beliefs in this book), but they must always be subservient to 'loving kindness'. In the paraphrased words of Pope Paul VI, our need for witnesses is greater than our need of teachers.

However, all this is not to confuse belief with *faith*. Faith is necessary and does matter, because faith is not an idea or a way of thinking - it is an attitude of trusting, of knowing that in our relationship with God, all will be well, and we will be loved and looked after: 'I will be with you always' says Jesus. And we reveal our faith, our trust and hope in God, by what we do, rather than what we believe. There is, of course, a relationship between be-lief and faith, but our contemporary world is far more interested in experiencing *fruits that will last*, rather than engaging in argu-ments about the number of angels on the proverbial pinhead. If we want to inspire a new generation to follow Christ, or at the very least ensure the church survives, then we need to under-stand anew the good news of the gospel.

This book is about not giving up on faith, even if you find it difficult to accept all the doctrines and rules that the church-es have built up over the last 2,000 years. You don't need to be 'religious' in any traditional sense to follow the teachings of Jesus. The following Nine Steps are an invitation to return to the words of the gospel and see how Christ welcomes all comers; anyone can 'do' Christianity - it's a big tent, and we are all invited.

Starting Out - A Pilgrimage Within

'Come and see'
(JOHN 1:39)

In the words of Pope Francis: 'A pilgrimage is a spiritual journey. We don't choose our destination; it is God drawing us into Himself. Something inside us simply yearns to go. We feel invited, even summoned.'

A pilgrimage is a journey, often to an unknown place, where an individual goes in search of a new or deeper meaning about themselves, others and God. It is often a search for wholeness, leading to personal change, and as St John Henry Newman said, 'to live is to change'.

In medieval England one of the most popular pilgrimages was from London to Walsingham in East Anglia. Pilgrims would travel the 121 miles, stopping en-route at wayside chapels and hospices which offered hospitality. After taking their shoes off at the aptly named Slipper Chapel they would walk the last mile barefoot.

Few of us today have the time or the energy to walk such a distance. However, this book invites the reader to embark on a 'Pilgrimage Within', a virtual pilgrimage. Rather than walking 121 miles, there are 121 chapters to read, organised into Nine Steps. I would recommend reading just one or two chapters a day, reflecting on each Gospel passage, and considering what Christ might be saying to you as you continue your journey. You might even wish to read the last page barefoot!

Each chapter begins with a short extract from the Gospel (if you have a New Testament you may wish to read the full extract at some point, but this is not essential). This then leads us into a deeper meditation on what the words might mean for us today. Finally, there is a short question to reflect on and perhaps pray about before you move on.

Take a look at the painting on the front cover of this book - it shows Christ and two of the disciples starting out on the road to Emmaus. In his gospel, Luke tells us the name of one of the disciples, Cleopas, but he doesn't tell us who the other traveller is. Perhaps we are the other one? Perhaps our pilgrimage route is also the road to Emmaus?

If you are ready to take a fresh look at the Gospel of Jesus then let this book be your guide on the journey. As Jesus said to the very first disciples ... 'Come and see'.

1

—

The Problem with Religion

*'The scribes and the Pharisees occupy the
chair of Moses... but do not be guided by what
they do: since they do not practice what they
preach. They tie-up heavy burdens and lay
them on men's shoulders, but will they lift a
finger to move them? Not they!'*
(MATTHEW 23:1-5)

A friend once said to me, 'You often say - *you will know
them by their fruits*, but the fruits of organised religion
throughout history have often been pain, guilt and
misery'. It's hard to disagree. Wars are fought in the name of
religion; people were burnt at the stake in the name of God
or tortured by the Inquisition because they held spiritual
beliefs which other people disagreed with (note that no-one
was ever sent to the Inquisition because they weren't doing
enough for the poor, or because they were failing to forgive
their neighbour). This prompted Blaise Pascal to utter these
words in the 17th century: 'Men never do evil so completely
and cheerfully as when they do it from religious conviction'.
Even in our modern Western democracies religious beliefs
polarise and divide people, often producing distrust rather
than fellowship. Such arguments often centre on Christian

theory rather than practice, the 'what' of Christianity, rather than the 'how'.

On an individual level many say that religion has ruined their lives, filling them with fear and guilt, and in some cases preventing them from living life to the full. Rather than lifting them up they see religion as a weight dragging them down; bad news rather than 'Good News'. We are often told to just attend church once a week and we'll eventually 'understand'. But we seldom do. And of course, for most young people the church has become both unappealing and irrelevant. In short, religion has often done the very opposite of what it professes to achieve. Perhaps the philosopher Martin Buber was right when he said, 'nothing hides the face of God better than religion!'

All of this is nothing new and should not surprise us. Jesus had his own troubles with religion. Matthew describes how Jesus vents his anger at the scribes and Pharisees, the established religious leaders of his day. He calls them 'serpents', a 'brood of vipers' and 'whitened sepulchres': they love to be feted and honoured, exalting in their self-importance and power. Concerned with petty regulations and trivialities and corrupted by wealth they cannot see the truth; rather than helping those in need they add to their burdens. Obsessed with ensuring a correct outward observance of religion they fail to see that the heart of all faith is an inner transformation founded on love. Jesus' instruction to his disciples was to 'follow me'. However we can sometimes spend so much time worshipping Jesus that we forget to follow him.

Like the Pharisees of old many religious people today are obsessed with judgementalism, often using religious texts such as the Bible or the Koran to justify treating women as second-class citizens, oppressing the gay community or advocating holy war or violence as a way of achieving 'God's will'. As Pope Francis has said, 'Fundamentalism is a sickness that is in all religions... Religious fundamentalism is not religious, because it lacks God. It is idolatry, like idolatry of money... We Catholics have some - and not some, many - who believe in the absolute truth and go ahead dirtying the other with calumny, with disinformation, and doing evil'. To the fundamentalist everything is black and white, those who disagree are enemies - there is no dialogue, no tolerance or openness - only judgmentalism, only 'us' and 'them'. Religion can truly bring out the best in people, but sadly also the worst. Many are turned off religion because many religious people are no more loving, forgiving or compassionate than anybody else, and in some cases are much worse.

Pope Francis has repeatedly condemned clericalism - when clergy stand aloof from the faithful, demanding deference and a childish spirit of obedience - describing it as the 'evil of clericalism... a really awful thing'. By doing this they hinder rather than promote the gospel. Priests, says the Pope, are not 'distributors of bottled oil' but anoint through 'dirtying our hands in touching the wounds, the sins and the worries of the people'.

Over the years we have taken 150 pages of the four gospel writers and created an enormous theological edifice of doctrine and dogma, rules and regulations. Much organised religion has been about rearranging beliefs like deck chairs on the Titanic, while the passengers jump into lifeboats and row away before the ship sinks. We have dreamt up ways of excluding people, of looking down on those in different 'tribes', of exerting power and oftentimes piling misery on the lives of ordinary people. The German theologian Dietrich Bonhoeffer warned about this when he wrote about the dangers of 'religionless Christianity'. We have taken a message that Jesus said could be understood by the smallest child and created something that baffles the learned.

In the end religion killed Jesus - the religious leaders of the day could not tolerate what he stood for. This crucifixion continues today in the many acts of indifference, disrespect and violence carried out by so many in the name of God. Unsurprisingly many have rejected the established churches, but in doing so they often 'throw the baby out with the bathwater'. Perhaps it is time for us to look afresh at the simple message of love, justice and compassion which Jesus gives us in the Gospel.

....

Am I ready to take a fresh look at the Gospel?

2

—

The Journey Begins

'Take nothing for the journey: neither staff,
nor haversack, nor bread, nor money; and let
none of you take a spare tunic.'
(LUKE 9:3)

Whatever our outlook on life, most of us, at times, feel a sense of frustration and dissatisfaction. A sense that something is missing, that all is not quite as it should be - a feeling of 'is this as good as it gets?' Psychologists argue that the traditional 'midlife crisis' can happen at any time, when people ask, 'what am I supposed to be doing with my life?', realising perhaps that 'we only get one shot at life and it's passing me by'. Some of us find ourselves standing at the crossroads all our lives, forever frozen, never venturing on a spiritual journey of discovery, never setting out to see if there could be something more.

When Jesus called his first disciples, they immediately dropped everything and followed him. It must have been an extraordinary event. I wonder if those disciples were searching for something more, disappointed perhaps with how their lives had turned out? Suddenly here was something different, someone different, and nothing in their lives would be the same again.

This book goes back to those words of Jesus in the gospel, the same words those first disciples heard. The invitation to respond is there for us too.

Perhaps you feel you've heard it all before, you've listened to the gospel, you've read it, you know what's there - you've 'been there, done that'. If that's the case, then we need to leave such preconceptions behind. Jesus says, 'Take nothing for the journey: neither staff nor haversack.' Maybe we have baggage we need to leave behind - weariness or disappointment, or for many of us, the selfishness of our ego, which constantly makes us fearful of change, which tells us to stay put, to risk nothing; the ego which tells me that I must hold on to 'my staff, my bread, my money'.

If we are honest, most of us are weighed down with burdens of one sort or another, that we have either chosen to carry, or that have been placed on us by others. Jesus says 'Come to me ... Yes, my yoke is easy and my burden light'. We are called to empty ourselves of such burdens and leave a space for God to fill. Jesus asks us to travel lightly. He tells the disciples that he is all they need for the journey - he asks them to leave the past behind and step out in faith. They don't know where they are going, but they don't care - they are ready for an adventure.

Martin Luther King said, 'Faith is taking the first step even when you don't see the whole staircase'. It takes courage to step out along the road. Our ego will tell us: 'what if so and so happens? surely it is risky to leave so much behind? why not take along that spare tunic, just in case?' We need an attitude of trust - to be vulnerable, and open to the promptings of the Spirit. Once we have laid our burdens down at the feet of Christ we can then begin to see our real, true self (not our false 'ego self'). This discovery is what St. Augustine meant when he said, 'You have made us for yourself, O Lord, and our heart is restless until it rests in you'. Our journey is, in a sense, a journey home to freedom.

Perhaps you have set out on this journey before and turned back; no matter, now is the time to begin again. The journey is everything, but you will never be alone in the steps you take - let the words of Jesus in this book be your guide along the way.

....

Are you ready to begin the journey?

3

—

Lemonade

*As he was walking by the Sea of Galilee he saw
two brothers, Simon, who was called Peter,
and his brother Andrew; they were making a
cast in the lake with their net, for they were
fishermen. And he said to them, 'Follow me and
I will make you fishers of men'. And they left
their nets at once and followed him.*
(MATTHEW 4:18-20)

When I was very young, before I started school, I used to go with my mum to visit my Nana once a week. Each time Nana would ask me if I wanted a glass of lemonade. This was kept in a large bottle under her sink, and only seemed to come out for my visits. It was as flat as a pancake, but I had never tasted lemonade before, and it was sweet and delicious. Later, when I started school, I was invited to my friend Peter's birthday party, and on arrival I was asked by his mum if I would like some lemonade. 'Yes please!' I replied enthusiastically. When she brought it to me I was amazed at the bubbles, and when I tasted it, it almost blew my head off! The fizzy feeling was amazing. I went home and told my mum about my mind-blowing experience, and she laughed saying, 'that's what lemonade is supposed to taste like!'

The message and person of Jesus so excited the early disciples that they just left their nets, and everything they had, and followed him - unsure of what might happen to them, or where he would lead them.

For many of us the Christian message has become like flat lemonade. Some have grown disillusioned with organised religion, many with good reason. The number of those identifying as Christian continues to decline year on year in the West, and Church attendance is plummeting. With a sharp decline in participation among young people some commentators are predicting that the Church as we know it will soon disappear.

Faith has become so watered down and sanitized it often ceases to have much impact on our day-to-day lives. Many are happy to embrace a nice safe Christianity, ignoring the challenges the gospel makes on us to radically alter our behaviour, eliminate our selfishness and reject the prevailing consumer lifestyle.

But Christianity is not a safe option - the early disciples were blown away by their encounter with Jesus. The Nine Steps that follow are about rediscovering, or perhaps finding for the first time, that 'fizz of faith'.

As I first discovered as a small child - when a person tastes real lemonade, they never want to go back to the flat stuff!

....

Do I have nets I need to leave behind?

STEP ONE

Who is God?

I used to live in Tokyo and I remember visiting the crib in my local church at Christmas. Mary, Joseph and Jesus were all Japanese, dressed in traditional kimonos and looking very different from the Western nativity scene I was used to.

No two people have the same image of God. In truth, your image of God perhaps says more about you and your faith journey than it says about him. God is generally portrayed as a father, but he can also be a mother - he has no gender or ethnicity (as I discovered in Japan). For many he is a figure of authority, distant and remote, for others he is a loving presence, constantly intervening in the world. For some the word 'God' itself is a problem they just can't get past.

In Step One we go back to basics and ponder some difficult questions. Does God exist, and how can we describe him? It has been argued that even posing such questions demonstrates a lack of faith or is dangerous. In the past the Church often discouraged such thinking, praising those who possessed 'unquestioning faith'. Such an approach is unhelpful. In the extracts that follow we will see that uncertainty can be a friend not an enemy. Not only is it honest and inevitable to question and doubt, it's actually the first step on our path to spiritual renewal.

4

—

Doubt is our friend

Then Jesus came with them to a small estate called
Gethsemane... He took Peter and the two sons of
Zebedee with him. And sadness came over him,
and great distress. Then he said to them, 'My soul
is sorrowful to the point of death. Wait here and
keep awake with me.' And going on a little further
he fell on his face and prayed. 'My Father', he said
'if it is possible, let this cup pass me by.'
(MATTHEW 26:36-39)

When I was a teenager I went to see Samuel Beckett's play 'Waiting for Godot', a story about two men waiting for 'Godot', someone who continually sends word that he will appear but who never turns up. It has been interpreted by some to be an allegory for God's absence, with Godot symbolising a salvation which is promised by religion, but never actually materialises. Whilst queuing to go in, my friend, an atheist, playfully told me that by the end of the evening I would have lost my faith! For a moment I was terrified - what would my life be like without my faith? As it happened, I didn't really understand the play, and my beliefs remained intact.

Our ideas about God inevitably change over the years. Looking back, I had a rather childlike faith - I felt threatened by doubt, afraid that I might lose something by asking questions and thinking deeply. I saw doubt as a weakness, a failure on my part, and even a sin. I couldn't begin to ask myself questions such as 'Does God exist?' Any deviation from orthodoxy was dangerous – far simpler to get my faith 'off the shelf', accept everything I was taught at school and in the pulpit and push uncomfortable questions to the back of my mind. I remember someone once warning me, 'if you question Church teaching in that area then who's to say what will come next? Pull that thread and the whole thing might unravel!' In other words, I shouldn't leave my comfort zone. The Church would do my thinking for me.

We love certainty but it is over-rated, in fact it might even be sinful! Certainty often results in religious fundamentalism which can lead to bigotry and intolerance, or in some cases a complete loss of belief. As we get older we realise that certainty can be the enemy of belief, not a faithful friend. Everyone has doubts, the most famous saints, and of course Jesus himself, in the Garden of Gethsemane before his crucifixion, and in his final hours on the cross. Many of the great saints and mystics such as St John of the Cross have spoken about doubt as the 'dark night of the soul', a period of time when God seems distant and, in many cases, just not there at all. St John is clear that this is not something to be avoided, but to be embraced as a stage leading towards an eventual deeper appreciation of the presence of God. In short, doubt is holy. It will come in God's own time and it often appears out of our control. The theologian Peter Enns describes doubt as 'divine tough love'. It is God trying to lead us to something deeper, 'life to the full', rather than just turning up at church and saying our bedtime prayers.

It is good to think and to question; the 'unexamined life' as Socrates said, is not a great one. It can be scary to have doubts because we imagine that we are moving away from God. In reality we are only moving away from our comfortable and established ideas about God – the God of our childhood, the God we have compartmentalised, the small God.

If we are honest with ourselves we can acknowledge our doubts, not just about God himself, but about the various doctrines and practices of the churches. God has given us a thinking brain in order to question, explore and ponder. In fact, in many ways, this stage of doubt and questioning is essential if we are to grow spiritually. Perhaps a deeper connection with God is only possible after a crisis of faith, some loss, failure or sense of emptiness. Something needs to shake us out of our complacency, out of an attitude that says, 'I've got this all figured out', and force us to seek something better, something bigger.

Certainty often gives way to doubt, and then doubt to calm acceptance. It is an acceptance that things are not quite as black and white as they once appeared. God is bigger, more loving and more generous than we ever imagined. Doubt can become our teacher, and in time, the springboard to a deeper friendship with God.

....

Is it time to leave my comfort zone and embrace doubt and uncertainty as 'friends'?

5

—

Do not be afraid

'There is no need to be afraid, little flock, for it has pleased your Father to give you the kingdom...'
(LUKE 12:32)

Are you afraid of God?

Apparently the two most powerful emotions in life are fear and love. We generally act out of one or the other, and this applies to religion too. I remember my parents telling me about a preacher they listened to many years ago, who gave them a 'hellfire and brimstone' sermon. They left the church very afraid. For centuries Christians have been told to fear the wrath and punishment of God; to hide their faces before a God who dished out divine retribution, and ultimately would be their judge and jury on the last day.

How did this happen? The Bible says we are made in the 'image and likeness of God' but often we make God in our own image and likeness. If we have been raised by a harsh and unforgiving parent for example, then we might equate our Father in heaven with anger and distance. If our parents didn't model God's love to us, then we might have grown up with a view of God as a punishing authority figure. Moreover, it has often suited states and churches to project an image of God that kept people fearful and 'in their place'.

Yet the Gospel shows us a different reality. Fear is the enemy of faith. If we are afraid it is hard to risk love, to make ourselves vulnerable and open up to others. Fear imprisons us, but Jesus says, 'Do not be afraid; only have faith' (Mark 5:36).

Our relationship with God is one of friendship and trust. In Isaiah we hear God saying: 'Do not be afraid, for I have redeemed you; I have called you by your name you are mine'. We may not always hear God's call to us, but it is there nonetheless, and each of us decides in our own way how to respond.

....

What image of God do I have?

6

—

Blind faith?

'Do you believe at last?'
(JOHN 16:31)

M any very clever people have tried to prove the existence of God, and many others have tried to definitively argue that there is no God. Both tasks are impossible and doomed to failure. Nothing I can say or write can prove that God exists (or vice versa).

All religion is a question of faith (trusting in something or someone even when you know you can't be certain), and faith is always linked to hope. Whether you believe in God or not you will show faith and hope throughout your life. Faith in the people who serviced and pilot the aircraft you fly in. Faith in the doctor who treats you. Faith that the letter you post will reach its destination. Faith that the person you're going to marry will stay with you forever.

However, this is never a blind or unrealistic faith. A couple, for example, will undoubtedly have evidence of their love for each other in the words, actions and experiences of their life together. Similarly, we know that there is evidence in the Gospels - parables and teaching that resonates with us and touches our hearts. We can also experience the love and care that God has for us in our day-to-day experiences of life (see Step Four of this book). So whilst there is no certainty, there is certainly plenty of evidence and experience to draw upon in our quest for a truth that makes sense.

We are in charge of our own reality, we make our own choices and choose our own thoughts, we decide what to believe and what to dismiss. The world around us, and the events we experience, don't necessarily change, but we can decide how to respond to them - and we can choose faith and trust as our response.

Faith almost always leads to hope and joy, and without it life loses a little colour and excitement. Jesus knew this when he said, 'Everything is possible for anyone who has faith'. Faith opens doors which scepticism closes. Jesus isn't really trying to prove anything in the gospel; he just wants us to experience love.

Our choice is either that leap of trust and faith or sitting on the side-lines, waiting for a certainty that doesn't exist. In effect, Jesus is saying to us, 'don't stand at the side of the pool – trust me, jump in, and see what happens'.

....

Jesus says, 'happy is the man who does not lose faith in me'. Are there ways in which I hold back from making that leap of faith, and placing my trust in God?

7

—

Knowledge

*'We all have knowledge'; yes, that is so, but
knowledge gives self-importance - it is love
that makes the building grow.*
(1 CORINTHIANS 8:1)

Ken Robinson recounts a story of a small girl totally ab-
sorbed in drawing a picture in her primary school lesson. The teacher wandered over and asked her what
she was drawing. The girl replied, 'I'm drawing a picture of
God'. The teacher was surprised and said 'But nobody knows
what God looks like. The girl said, 'They will in a minute'.

If you are looking for certainty, then close this book now.
As someone once said, 'If anyone tells you they have all the
answers to everything then run a mile'. The world is full of
people promising 'instant enlightenment' or writing self-help
books on 'Happiness Now!' Some claim to have a hotline to
God which no one else possesses, or a special insight which
no one else has received. Anyone who claims to know it all,
probably knows very little. Far better to listen to those who
say they are often groping in the dark, who see shades of grey
not black and white, who speak in parables and metaphor
rather than certainty and dogma.

The letters of a great saint such as Mother Teresa reveal a person often afflicted by doubt, uncertainty and confusion. Faith cannot really exist without uncertainty, otherwise it cannot be called faith. Mother Teresa's lack of certainty enhances rather than diminishes her work with the poor, and her decision to see the presence of God in the unloved and uncared for. Knowing that our saints are mere mortals with their own demons, rather than superhuman founts of all wisdom, allows us to accept our own limitations and confusion. And the deeper a person goes spiritually the more they are at home with ambiguity and nuance.

The knowledge we acquire from theology textbooks and catechisms is far less important than the truth that our lived experience reveals - our relationships, our setbacks and moments of light, our joy and pain. In the words of the Franciscan theologian Fr Richard Rohr, 'The only things we know at any deep and real level are the things we have personally experienced'. A faith based only on *right beliefs* is built on weak foundations – it is *right relationships* that usher in the kingdom of heaven, or as Paul says that 'make the building grow'. The role of theology is not to create an intellectually satisfying set of correct beliefs, it is to set out an authentic and compelling vision of the Christian life.

If faith is purely intellectual, based on knowing stuff and believing in things then we have climbed aboard a dangerous boat. As we get older we will encounter arguments that punch holes in this craft of knowledge - there will always be someone cleverer than we are, ready to tell us our arguments are faulty. Like St Peter we need to step out of the boat and just trust - we then stop stressing about having a correct set of beliefs and give control to God. It now becomes less about us, and all about God taking care of us (perhaps this is what Jesus meant when he said you have to lose your life in order to gain it).

One of the greatest theologians to have ever lived, St Thomas Aquinas author of the 'Summa Theologica', had a mystical experience towards the end of his life whilst saying mass. After this he stopped all his writing, saying 'Everything I have written seems like straw by comparison with what I have seen and what has been revealed to me'.

The anonymous 14th century author of the spiritual classic, 'The Cloud of Unknowing' (probably a Carthusian monk from Nottingham), wrote that, 'All these images and thoughts and ideas and doctrines about God are really good, but we all know that the infinite God can never be limited to any image, thought or idea.'

My friend, a committed atheist, delights in telling me that he doesn't believe in 'an old man with a grey beard sitting on a cloud in the sky peering down at his creation.' I annoy him by replying that, 'I also don't believe in the God that you don't believe in!' God cannot be pinned down. He does not belong to anyone, he is not located in any one place. He is not found only in one religion, one church or one way of thinking. Whenever we try and put 'his ways' into words (or draw him!) or attempt to grasp the depth of his love for us, our human ways of thinking fail us. Try defining 'infinity' for example... it's impossible! A student once told me, 'I can't get my head round God', and I could see where he was coming from. Certainty is the enemy of faith. If you are certain, then by definition, you have no need of faith.

In the fourth century Gregory of Nyssa criticised those who thought that Christianity consisted solely in 'doctrinal precision'. Faith is not an intellectual assent to a series of doctrines - it is becoming aware that God is close at hand, by our side and on our side, and ready to connect with us. The faith we have is faith in God, not a set of religious beliefs.

Belief in God is not an exercise of the mind. Just as we can know *about* someone (for example, the Prime Minister) and not 'know' them personally, so we can claim to know all about God, and yet not *know* him. Knowing about something in our head, and actually knowing someone in our hearts are two very different things. And the journey from head to heart can be a long one.

It's fine not to know everything. It's OK not to be a know-all. Far from limiting a person, this outlook enables us to become more comfortable with ourselves, less anxious and more tolerant of difference.

God is both so far beyond our human understanding and yet at the same time closer to us than we can ever imagine. The One who made fathomless galaxies and billions of stars has numbered every hair on our head. We don't need to pretend to know everything, we just need to know one thing - God is closer than we think.

....

How comfortable am I with uncertainty and ambiguity?

8

—

God is not a Christian!

Then Peter addressed them: 'The truth I have now come to realise' he said 'is that God does not have favourites, but that anybody of any nationality who fears God and does what is right is acceptable to him.'
(ACTS 10:34-35)

Many places in the world describe themselves as 'God's Own Country'. In Britain, Yorkshire is often described as 'God's Own County'. As someone born and bred in Lancashire I might dispute that! Throughout history, certain groups and nations have declared themselves as special in God's eyes or thought that they were favoured by God over other groups. German soldiers even had belt buckles inscribed with the phrase 'God is with us' (and presumably not with those they were trying to kill).

If you think God is a Catholic or an Anglican then you are mistaken. He isn't a Muslim or a Hindu either. We can't pin labels on God, he is not a tribal or sectarian deity; too often organised religions make God absurdly small and petty in order to fit their own prejudices and small-mindedness. There is no contradiction between being a Christian and accepting the notion that God can reveal himself in other ways and in other faiths.

Jesus himself was a Jew. The religion based on his teachings - Christianity - came later. Jesus preached the Gospel to all-comers - to the hated Samaritans, to the Pharisees and scribes, to the lowly and dispossessed - no one was excluded because of their background or prior beliefs. The Gospel is for all peoples, in all places, at all times. The workings of the Holy Spirit are never confined to any one person, nation, Christian denomination or faith group. The Spirit blows where it wants and when it wills. If we think that our particular ways are somehow superior to everyone else's, if we look down on others, if we are exclusive rather than inclusive, then that is to embrace the pride and arrogance that Jesus was at such pains to attack in the religious leaders of his day. They were so concerned with preserving their own power and prestige that they couldn't see the Truth when it was standing in front of them.

No one group has a monopoly on holiness or love, no one person has a special hot-line to God that no-one else can access. What does God want? He wants to share himself with us, with the whole of creation - a loving relationship that is open to everyone and freely given. This isn't theology - it's common sense.

Our loving Father is father to all; as St Peter said, 'God has no favourites'. No matter who you are, where you are from, or what you have done, God sees you as his beloved child.

Do I harbour in my heart the idea that 'my way is the only way'? Do I look down on others who are different?

9

—

False gods

'You shall have no gods except me.'
(EXODUS 20:3)

It has been said that we end up worshipping whatever we focus our attention on. The first commandment states that we shall not have false gods before us. The obvious false gods are of course: money, house, car and possessions, and involve worship in the shopping centre or on-line. For some it is career, celebrity or status - worshipping at the altar of our own ego. For others it is the perfect body or super fitness - the gym replacing the chapel.

How many of us worship at the altar of the TV, smartphone or computer? A recent report found that US teenagers spend an average of 7 hours and 22 minutes on their phone *each day* (not including time spent on homework). A UK survey polled 2,000 adults and found that the average person will spend the equivalent of 34 years of their lives staring at screens (phones, laptops and TVs).

The old saying, 'home is where the heart is', tells us that wherever or whatever we feel connected to, is our home. Jesus told the disciples to, 'Make your home in me, as I make mine in you'. So, take time today to lift your eyes from the screen, or from whatever it is you focus on, and come to rest awhile in your spiritual home. Switching our focus to God, no matter how briefly (often it is just a word or glance) almost always leads to the desire to focus on our neighbour too. The message of the Gospel is that our relationships are more important than the things we briefly possess, and the technology that sometimes possesses us.

Where do I focus my attention?

10

—

Why have you deserted me?

'My God, my God, why have you deserted me?'
(MATTHEW 27:47)

The Holocaust survivor, Elie Wiesel, in his book 'The Trial of God' recounts an event he witnessed in the Auschwitz death camp during World War II. Some of the Jewish prisoners put God on trial (in his absence) for the crime of abandoning his people. Prisoners spoke for the defence and prosecution - those in favour of a guilty verdict argued that God had stood by and done nothing when faced with the murder of millions of Jews and others in the Nazi Holocaust. At the end of the trial God was found guilty.

When Jesus is crucified he cries out, 'My God, why have you deserted me?' There is a real hopelessness in his words, he feels abandoned - where is God in his hour of greatest need? In all his other prayers (and this is a prayer), Jesus uses the term Father (or 'Abba') rather than God. On the cross he feels the Father's absence, but he knows, deep down, He is still there - Jesus is still able to pray, but not quite in the same intimate way as before. Like many of us at certain times in our lives, Jesus is struggling to feel the Father's presence.

There are many theological explanations as to why bad things happen to good people, but they are rarely of any use when a person is going through terrible pain and hardship. In such circumstances words are rarely helpful, and often appear as insensitive or worse still, pious platitudes.

Sometimes when we are faced with unimaginable pain, doubt or darkness the only thing we can do is echo Jesus' prayer on the cross, and trust that one day we will receive an answer. Interestingly, Elie Wiesel records that once the guilty verdict was given in Auschwitz, there was a period of silence, and 'Then we went to pray'.

The truth is that Jesus embraces his humanity on the cross; he does not shirk from the suffering, desolation and forsaken-ness that all humans experience. On the cross he takes on board our woundedness and pain, and in our times of suffering we are closer to Christ than we can perhaps ever imagine. Our pain is Christ's pain, and his is ours. In his memoir 'Night', Wiesel describes how a much-loved boy was hanged at Auschwitz. The young boy weighed hardly anything - his size didn't afford him a quick end, and he struggled for a while before death eventually came. The other prisoners were forced to stand and watch in horror. Wiesel writes: 'Behind me, I heard a man asking, "Where is God now?" And I heard a voice within me answer him "Where is He? Here he is. He is hanging here on this gallows." '

11

—

The Prodigal Son

'he was lost and is found.'
(LUKE 15:24)

Whatever our age we are all just grown-up children, and we love a good story. That's why Jesus speaks in parables - a powerful way of revealing truth through story-telling. We can forget a series of bullet point propositions but once heard, the parable of the Prodigal Son is never forgotten. It is a story that tells us exactly who God is.

A father has two sons. The youngest goes off with his share of his father's inheritance and squanders his money on 'a life of debauchery', leaving him destitute, working on a pig farm. He resolves to return to his father, beg forgiveness and ask to be treated as a paid servant. On his return he tells his father what has happened and says he no longer deserves to be called his son. But the father forgives him and prepares a feast in his honour. The elder son is furious at the father's generosity and refuses to join in the celebrations. However, the father reassures him, and tells him to rejoice, 'your brother here was dead and has come to life; he was lost and is found.'

This is a simple story, but it speaks truth to all of us. We are often the prodigal son - foolishly squandering the gifts the Father has given us, thinking only of ourselves and wanting to go our own way. The Father doesn't stop us, he lets us go, then waits at the bedroom window, each day looking out and hoping that one day we might return. And when we understand the error of our ways, return and ask for forgiveness there is nothing but joy and acceptance. Forgiveness comes quickly, love conquers all.

This illustrates a universal and neglected truth. We often grow in wisdom not from our 'spiritual success stories' but through our sinfulness, failure and suffering. The prodigal son creates a totally new loving relationship with his father after his disastrous life choices have led him to a dead end. The last shall be first; there is hope for us all.

But why does Jesus include an elder brother in the story? On one level the parable would have worked fine without him.

The elder brother represents all those negative, petty thoughts, jealousies and resentments we often harbour. He considered himself to be the perfect son, but inwardly he seethes with resentment and cannot forgive. Maybe we too are thinking 'yes, that's just not fair!' But God's loving mercy is abundant and doesn't conform to our narrow judgmentalism. There is always the chance of a fresh start with God; always accepting, always forgiving.

....

What happens when God sees you? Pause for a moment and consider Jesus' explanation in this parable, words you were meant to hear and take to heart: 'While he was still a long way off, his father saw him and was moved with pity. He ran to the boy, clasped him in his arms and kissed him tenderly.'

12

—

Hell, fire and brimstone

'You ████████████ ████ 'You must love your n████ ████ hate your enemy. But I say this to you: love your enemies and pray for those who persecute you; in this way you will be sons of your Father in heaven, for he causes his sun to rise on bad men as well as good, and his rain to fall on honest and dishonest men alike.'
(MATTHEW 5: 43-46)

When I was in primary school I remember being taught about 'mortal sins'. I was told that such sins would lead me to eternal damnation in the fires of Hell (unless of course I repented before I died and received forgiveness and absolution). It was a terrifying concept. Even missing church on Sunday without good reason or telling lies could be a mortal sin. I vividly remember walking home after the lesson, wondering if I had committed any mortal sins, and if I were knocked down and killed by a car without the opportunity to confess, would I be destined for eternal punishment? I was afraid, but even at that age I remember thinking that much of this just didn't make sense.

It was a product of a church that was perhaps more interested in power and control, and less concerned with

teaching   the healing and unconditional love of
God for h   en.

When   ch older I managed to persuade a very angry perso   seek revenge on someone who had wronged
him by   ave vengeance to God'. He was quite religious a   urn of phrase' seemed to calm him down.
What I   scuss with him was my belief that God isn't
interes   eaking vengeance or settling old scores.

This is just not who God is. How have we ended up with
a Jesus who forgives abundantly in the gospels but punishes
eternally in the next life? Why do we find it so hard to believe
in a God of mercy and compassion? Perhaps it is because it
just doesn't seem fair. Our lives (and the foreign policy of
our nation-states) are ruled by ideas of retribution and justice - by this we mean that people get punished for stepping
out of line. It's how the world operates, and we like it! We
are brought up with this from an early age and we hate it
when somebody 'gets away with it'. Hollywood films follow
a familiar trajectory - the 'baddy' appears to get off scot-free
initially, but in the end they get their 'just desserts' and we
cheer! Woe betide any director who lets the 'bad guy' get
away unpunished.

For many older Christians brought up on a diet of 'hellfire
and brimstone' it is part of our mindset. Hence so many of us
fear God, we fear his wrath and vengeance, and we fear death.
We simply cannot understand a God who is all-embracing
love and forgiveness. We seem to need and understand hell
much more than God does! We remember our childhood images of hell far more easily than the promise of eternal life
with a God who loves us.

Of course whilst Jesus came to show us how to create
the kingdom of heaven on earth, many people create hell for
themselves here and now by their actions. If we choose to

do wrong then the consequences for us are invariably pain, discomfort and suffering in this life. But as for eternal damnation and suffering in hell? Well let's leave all that to the infinite mercy and love of God. For when Christ conquered death and rose from the dead he did it for everyone.

....

Can I accept for myself the eternal mercy and
forgiveness of a God who loves me?

13

Don't ask God to love you more

When I was a child, I used to talk like a child, and think like a child, and argue like a child, but now I am a man, all childish ways are put behind me.
(1 CORINTHIANS 13:11)

When I was a child I remember praying that God would draw closer to me. I saw him in the way many children do, as a grandfather figure, far away in the highest heavens, sitting on a cloud and watching me. In my prayers I would ask him to be with me, to come down from the cloud and help me out. I would often have a shopping list of requests for his consideration, things for him to do (if he had a spare moment). I would regularly remind him of the list in case he had forgotten what I had said on previous occasions.

St Paul says, 'When I was a child I used to talk like a child, and think like a child'. Perhaps we need to stop asking God to draw closer to us - he can't get any closer! We can't suddenly 'achieve' the presence of God because we have always been in the presence of God. We don't 'find' God, he was never lost. As St Augustine said, 'God is closer to your soul than you are yourself'. In other words don't ask God to love you more - you can't be loved any more. Perhaps we need to pray for the awareness to see just how beloved we are, and then act on that knowledge to love others. As St John Chrysostom put it, 'God is everywhere. You decide whether you are close to him or not.'

As a child I thought that if I did good things then God would like me more, instead of realising that if I did good things I'd like myself more! God's love is not dependent on us doing XYZ; God loves us so that we are then able to do XYZ.

Whether we are conscious of it or not we are living in his presence. Jesus came to show us the extraordinary truth that God transcends everything, and at the same time lives in completeness within each person. By nature of our birth we are connected to God (whether we like it or not), and our life journey is not so much to realise who we will become, but to become aware of who we already are.

....

Do I need to change the way I think?

14

—

The Vineyard

'Why be envious because I am generous?'
(MATTHEW 20:16)

There is something to annoy everyone in the parable of the vineyard labourers! Jesus says the kingdom of heaven is like a landowner hiring workers for his vineyard. After agreeing to pay each person one denarius a day, he continues to hire new people, including some at the 'eleventh hour' of the day. When he comes to pay them, all are given the same one denarius, which leads the ones hired first to grumble and complain - why should they be paid the same as those who only did an hour's work? The landowner replies, 'Why be envious because I am generous?'

This just doesn't seem fair, and if we had done a 12-hour shift in the 'scorching heat' we would probably have seen the landowner's behaviour as outrageous. But God's ways are not our ways. God's love for us knows no bounds and doesn't conform to our conventions of justice. It is freely given to all in equal measure, those who are cradle Christians and those who come late to the party, those who worship every Sunday and those who never darken the door of a church, those who shout 'Lord, Lord!' and those who don't. God has a generous love beyond all our understanding, and all our human notions of fairness and 'what is right'. Jesus is telling his followers that this unlimited love is the love that keeps on giving, there is no end to it - it cannot be earned by hard work and gritting our teeth, it's freely given to all, 'pressed down and running over'.

The needs of those who arrive late to the vineyard are no less than those who got there early. They all have families to feed and bills to pay - the landowner asks the workers to look with solidarity at their brothers and sisters, and be grateful for his benevolence. Similarly, God knows what we need, and he is prepared to be generous to all in his giving.

Our ego-driven selves always seem to want love to be 'earned' rather than freely given. But God's love cannot be measured out like this; his love is always total, and one person will never receive more than another. Of course, this is a gift and we are free to walk away from God. But this parable tells us that even if we come back to him at the 'eleventh hour' the fullness of his love will be given to us. Thus 'the last will be first.'

. . . .

We can often agree with parables like this in our heads, whilst our hearts scream 'no way!' This is only human. It's only when we start putting these ideas into practice that we will know if we really believe them, and know if we have really changed...

Can I see myself in solidarity with my neighbour rather than in competition? Can I rejoice in God's generosity rather than grumbling about 'fairness'?

15
—

The Word of God?

The word of God is something alive and active...
(HEBREWS 4:12)

If you've ever been in the House of Commons at
Westminster you might have seen the Hansard reporters
in the balcony above the Speaker's chair. Their job is to
record for posterity every word that is said in the chamber.
It's exhausting work and they are replaced every ten minutes
or so, but the result is an accurate historical document of
what has been said and by whom.

Each section of this book begins with an extract from the
Bible, and it's important to say at the outset that the 'Good
Book' isn't Hansard. It doesn't attempt to be a literal historical
document, and God certainly didn't 'dictate' it to the authors.
The Bible was written by human beings – it reveals their views
and opinions, which are not necessarily the same as God's.

However, we shouldn't assume that something cannot be
true unless it is a historical fact. As Peter Keenan points out
in 'The Birth of Jesus the Jew', the Bible is 'not history, in
the sense that it has come to be understood in the modern
world, which too often assumes that something is true only
if it is at the same time factual'.

The Bible had about forty main contributors, and some of the 'books' in there are actually collections of writings from several authors. Much of this writing is metaphor and parable, which often illuminates some aspect of God *without necessarily being literally true*. This is especially true in the Old Testament and is certainly the case with the creation stories in Genesis. Science, and Darwin in particular, have shown us that the world was not literally made in seven days (and Eve was not made from Adam's rib). All things were and are created by God, but over billions of years. Similarly, some things just make little sense - for example God supposedly tells Moses that 'you are not to wear a garment made from two kinds of fabric' (Leviticus 19:19). Worse still Elisha, when he is jeered at by some small boys who call him a 'baldhead', apparently curses them in the name of God, and forty-two of the boys are immediately savaged by some bears who emerge from a wood! (2 Kings 2: 23-25).

This isn't the handiwork of God, it is a product of a human writer creating God in his own image with all the flawed misconceptions of his time and place. If scripture (or any minister or faith) portrays God as violent, oppressive or vengeful then this tells you more about them than it does about God. In America slave-owners would frequently justify their actions by referring to Paul's letter to the Ephesians 6:5, 'slaves be obedient to your masters... as unto Christ'. In our own day the Bible is still wheeled out to oppress women and gay people. So, if parts of the Bible make you cross then you are in good company. In fact it's often been said that the best book to read if you want to become an atheist is the Bible! That may be going a bit too far but it's certainly true that an angry God who decides it's a good idea to drown every creature he has created (apart from Noah and a selection of lucky animals) is not one I can believe in.

We must be careful in describing the Bible as the definitive, once and for all, 'Word of God' for this suggests that everything in it is infallibly true and this makes no sense. It also suggests that God suddenly starts speaking to us at certain points in history and then stops, when in fact God speaks to us all the time through everything he has created. In the words of the comedienne Gracie Allen, 'never place a period where God has placed a comma'. God hasn't stopped speaking to us and never will. The Bible is less instruction manual, and more an opportunity to learn deep wisdom and compassion.

For Christians, the New Testament is the most important part of the Bible. The New Covenant is created - Christ shows us in clear and vivid terms how we can be in a living relationship with God. The four Gospels were probably written between 30 and 80 years after Jesus' death and are the product of oral and written testimonies from a variety of sources, a combination of faith, recollection and metaphor. Certain events are mentioned in some of the Gospels which are not mentioned in others, and in places the writers produce different interpretations of the same event. The gospel texts are not a history textbook or some kind of Biblical Hansard, and the writers did not view them in that way. The important element for example in the Feeding of the Five Thousand is not the number of people fed – it is the message that Jesus is the bread of life who nourishes his people. This message is true whatever may or may not have taken place on a specific day in history. We can believe the event described is historical, but the message goes beyond 'what happened, when'. The truth always goes beyond a text - the gospels are sacramental; they speak to our hearts. This is why we return to read them again and again, often seeing in them something new that we didn't discern on our first or twenty first reading!

Inspired by the Spirit, the Gospel writers (and while we are at it many other authors of religious texts) attempt to teach, to pass on faith, to enlighten and to convert. Like any good writer or poet their purpose is to wake us up, to inspire us to believe in the Good News - to have faith in the person of Jesus and in his message. The Gospel is not there just to be read, like a good novel. We must do something with it, we have to be the change that we read. It's not there to entertain us or provide us with a historical book of facts, it's there to transform us, to inspire us to action, to give us a new heart. And of course, the gospels contain only a snapshot of all the many things Jesus did in his lifetime. As John said right at the end of his gospel:

> 'There were many other things that Jesus did; if all were written down, the world itself, I suppose, would not hold all the books that would have to be written.'

....

Can I see scripture as sacrament? Can I be the change that I read?

16
—

We are all 'Doubting Thomas'

Then he spoke to Thomas, 'Put your finger here; look, here are my hands. Give me your hand; put it into my side. Doubt no longer but believe'. Thomas replied, 'My Lord and my God!' Jesus said to him: 'You believe because you can see me. Blessed are those who have not seen and yet believe.'
(JOHN 20:27-29)

Step One of this book is all about acknowledging the existence of doubt and uncertainty in life. No-one should feel guilty or ashamed of doubt. It is part of being human. John tells us that after Jesus rose from the dead he comes back to see his disciples, but Thomas isn't there, and does not believe the others when they say they have seen him. Like Thomas we often doubt what we cannot see and touch. Yet Jesus does not reject Thomas because of his unbelief. He comes back for him. In a sense Jesus continually comes back for us too, reminding us that he is on our side, rooting for us - he is in our corner. Although we can sometimes stop believing in God, He never stops believing in us.

It is interesting to note that Christ returns after his resurrection with his wounds still visible. It is almost as if he is saying to Thomas, 'we are all wounded, we are all hurt, but the resurrection is here for everyone too'. After woundedness comes new life.

If you, like Thomas, have doubts then the verse in 1 John 4:12 is worth considering: *'No one has ever seen God; but if we love one another, God lives in us and his love is made complete in us'*. Pause for a moment and read that again, it is one of the most significant verses in the Bible. Through our love for each other we allow God to become real and tangible, thereby enabling Him to make his home in us. In this way we are, in John's words, 'blessed', because we have not seen and yet believe.

We are to be God's presence in the world. St Teresa of Avila said: 'Christ has no body now but yours. No hands, no feet on earth but yours. Yours are the eyes through which he looks compassion on this world. Yours are the feet with which he walks to do good. Yours are the hands through which he blesses all the world'.

Whether we have a faith or not, whenever we show love to others we make God manifest in the world, and more than that, we enable his love to be complete, to be perfected. It is why we are here.

What work can God do now through me?

17

—

Where do I start?

It is God, for his own loving purpose, who
puts both the will and the action into you.
(PHILIPPIANS 2:13)

You might be saying, 'I would like to know God better, but where do I start? How do I begin to connect more deeply with God?' If this is a thought you have had then it might be helpful to understand that it is a desire (or a 'will') which has been put there first by God. The desire to know him more, comes from him.

It is often when we are at our lowest ebb that we find ourselves searching for something beyond ourselves. When we feel separate from God we often experience dissatisfaction, something often hard to pin down, but real nonetheless. It's like a piece of the jigsaw puzzle is missing, something that completes us is not there. If God lives in us then the root of our search for him is already within; our desire for him is an echo or a reflection of his first call to us. It is a comfort to know that the very *desire* to get closer to God comes from him, and shows us just how important we are to him.

God is constantly reaching out to us, searching for our response. Hence the thoughts and questions that spur us on in our quest come from him. He knocks on the door first.

As St John of the Cross put it, 'In the first place it should be known that if a person is seeking God, his Beloved is seeking him much more.' Everyone who genuinely asks and wants to see the way to God will be shown.

Is it possible for me to see that the yearning I have for something more, is an invitation, placed in my heart by God himself?

18

—

Choices

*The apostles said to the Lord, 'Increase
our faith'.*
(LUKE 17:5)

Non-belief is becoming increasingly popular in western countries according to a recent British Social
Attitudes survey. Half of the UK population say
they do not belong to any religion. Since 1983 the number of
people who state that they are Christian has nearly halved
from 66% to 35%. One in four members of the public stated,
'I do not believe in God', compared to one in ten in 1998.
Atheists claim that you cannot prove God exists, so belief is
an illusion.

Given this apparent decline in religion it is worth examin-
ing how Jesus, and later the twelve apostles persuaded people to embrace faith. Jesus never really sets out to prove anything as such. What he did was to persuade people that what
he said made sense. His words and actions resonated with
his listeners. He offered no definitive 'cast iron' proof, he just
said 'this is how you should live your life'. He offered them
a way of living based on loving relationships. His followers
made a choice, they said, 'yes this makes sense to me, this is
something I can follow, something I can believe in'.

Jesus says that God is not a theological concept to be proven but a Person to be loved and followed. As we come to the end of the First Step on our virtual pilgrimage it is worth reflecting on the choices we all must face at some point in our lives: does the Gospel of Love make sense to me? Can I see myself trying to follow this Way? Do I think it might bring me a sense of peace? Will it give my life and my relationships meaning and fulfilment? Might it free me from worry and anxiety, and make sense of my suffering?

In the Second Step we shall look in more detail at who Jesus was, and the choices he offers us.

....

Am I ready to make a choice?

STEP TWO

Who is Jesus?

There were dozens of messiahs, prophets and holy men around in Jesus' day. Some had small bands of followers but once these leaders died their groups tended to fizzle out fairly quickly. Jesus was different. After his death his movement exploded and eventually spread to every corner of the globe. Today Christianity is the world's largest religion with 2.4 billion followers. Leaving aside your personal views about Jesus, from a purely historical perspective this is an astonishing phenomenon.

There can be little doubt that a person called Jesus existed, but who exactly was he, and what was his message? This Second Step examines what Jesus says in various extracts from the gospel and explores what these words might mean for us today. In taking this step we may need to leave behind some of our old preconceptions about who Jesus was and perhaps meet him again for the first time?

19

—

Who is Jesus?

The word was made flesh, he lived among us...
(JOHN 1:14)

Most historians can agree that a person called Jesus existed. There is a mass of evidence to show that someone of this name lived and became quite famous. Roman and Jewish historians write about him and there are thousands of references to him in Greek and Latin manuscripts, and in the writings of the early Church Fathers. The question is not 'did he exist?', but 'who was he?'

First, the easy bit - Jesus was a man. The gospel writers tell us he was 'born of a woman', and brought up and looked after as a small child, learning things from his parents. He generally did what his mother asked him to do. Like us, he needed to eat and drink. He got tired and needed sleep. He had to work. He got sad, and occasionally he showed anger. He made close friendships with some, and was ridiculed and rejected by others. He was tempted. He suffered pain and at the age of thirty three, he died. It is fascinating that Jesus refers to himself as 'the son of man' over 80 times in the gospels. It's almost as if he is stressing the fact that he is flesh and blood, one of us, a human being. The churches have often been guilty of downplaying or ignoring Jesus' humanity, it is always 'son of God' that appears in our worship and creeds.

The Gospel writers whilst describing Jesus' humanity, also point us towards his divinity. They report how he performed extraordinary deeds - healing the sick, giving sight to the blind and raising Lazarus from the dead. His teaching touched the hearts of many his listeners, there was a wisdom to his words that captivated and inspired his followers, and thousands came to see him preach. He claimed to forgive sins (which only God can do). Many of his listeners were outraged at this and wanted him put to death as a blasphemer. He fulfilled hundreds of prophecies made about him many years beforehand. Finally, the gospel records that he rose from the dead.

The Gospel writers tell us that Jesus was conscious of his divinity. He says: 'I am the Way, the Truth and the Life', and tells the disciples - if you want to know God then you can discover him 'through me'. He says, 'I am the Light of the World', and promises eternal life: 'whoever believes in me will never die'. At the Last Supper he says, 'To have seen me is to have seen the Father'. When Jesus says, 'The Father and I are one', John records that the Jews 'fetched stones to stone him'. When Jesus asks them why, they reply, 'you are only a man and you claim to be God'. After Jesus is arrested and brought before the high priest he is asked, 'Are you the Christ, the Son of the Blessed One?' Jesus replies, 'I am'. This reply sealed his fate in the eyes of the Jews as a blasphemer. The gospel writers are clear that Jesus says things about himself that left his hearers in no doubt that he was claiming to be the Son of God.

So why does Jesus almost always refer to himself as the son of man, rather than the Son of God? He is saying to us, 'I am one of you; this is how you should live as a man or a woman'. When we emphasise his status as Son of God rather than son of man then it's an easy next step to say that being like Jesus is nigh on impossible. So we often give up. But Jesus in effect tells his disciples, 'no, you can be like this too!'

Although we can be very confident that a man called Jesus existed, we cannot prove that he was also divine. That is a matter of faith. Yet for billions of people *he is* the doorway through which we can see the love of God, enabling us not just to *know* about God, but to *experience* that love in our daily life. For the Christian, following Jesus is about receiving and passing on the transforming power of love from a God who became like us, and in doing so, taught us how to live.

Who is Jesus for me?

20
—
We all follow something or someone

When he went out...he noticed a tax collector,
Levi by name, sitting by the customs house,
and said to him, 'Follow me'. And leaving
everything he got up and followed him.
(LUKE 5:27-28)

Perhaps, like me, you follow a football club. My team, Preston North End, inspires great devotion in its followers, and this is the case for almost every club in the world. It's a lifelong pursuit and often involves obsession and passion; Diego Maradona said, 'football isn't a game, nor a sport, it's a religion'. Others may follow a political party or ideology such as socialism; for some it's the nation state – 'my country, right or wrong'. In an age of social media many follow celebrities - the footballer Cristiano Ronaldo has the most popular Instagram account in the world with over 520 million followers. Some follow music or fashion trends, styling themselves on fashion icons, adopting their image and wearing the clothes they promote. Others are pre-occupied with the stock market, religiously following the FTSE and Dow Jones, buying and selling shares to enhance their portfolio. Even those people who say they follow no-one and nothing, will still have a philosophy or moral code they adhere to, even if it's just 'Looking after Number One'.

Jesus asked Levi, more commonly known as the disciple Matthew, to follow him. Matthew was a tax collector. He would have been wealthy and probably of some importance in the local government. Most of society at that time considered tax collectors dishonest and corrupt, abusing their authority by siphoning off part of the tax take for themselves. In spite of, or perhaps because of this, Jesus calls him. In an instant, and leaving everything behind, Matthew gets up and follows him and his life is changed forever.

Later Jesus goes to eat at Matthew's home. The Pharisees complain about him dining with tax collectors, and Jesus' reply is simple: 'It is not those who are well who need the doctor, but the sick'. Acknowledging our own sickness, our own need of a 'doctor' is an important first step on our journey. We too need healing.

Jesus' invitation to follow him applies to everyone, everywhere, in every age. He comes to us whoever we are, and meets us wherever we are.

Perhaps we might consider the advice of the Jesuit theologian Fr Pierre Teilhard de Chardin: 'Instead of standing on the shore and proving to ourselves that the ocean cannot carry us, let us venture on its waters just to see.'

....

Who or what do I follow?

21

—

Mission Statement

He stood up to read, and they handed him the scroll of the prophet Isaiah. Unrolling the scroll he found the place where it is written: 'The spirit of the Lord has been given to me, for he has anointed me. He has sent me to bring the good news to the poor, to proclaim liberty to captives and to the blind new sight, to set the downtrodden free, to proclaim the Lord's year of favour.' He then rolled up the scroll, gave it back to the assistant and sat down. And all eyes in the synagogue were fixed on him. Then he began to speak to them, 'This text is being fulfilled today even as you listen'.

(LUKE 4:17-22)

These days mission statements are all the rage. Most companies and organisations, even schools, are encouraged to have one. They are supposed to provide a sense of vision and purpose, to summarise what the organisation is, and what it hopes to do. Prime Ministers and Presidents, on taking office, will generally outline their 'mission' in their first speech - their hopes for the future and the way they intend to govern.

So here is Jesus' mission statement. He returns to Nazareth, his hometown, and goes to the synagogue on the Sabbath day. Luke records that these are the first words Jesus speaks in public - his first sermon if you will. He reads from Isaiah, saying he has been sent to proclaim freedom for prisoners, give sight to the blind and set the oppressed free. Interestingly, he misses off the last line of the reading from Isaiah which is *'a day of vengeance for our God.'* For Jesus, God is compassion not vengeance.

At first glance we might think - there's nothing here for me and move on. Many of Jesus' listeners did. And yet ... how many of us are *prisoners* of our own habits and lifestyle, enslaved by our pursuit of 'false gods' such as money or status? How many of us are *blind* to the suffering of our neighbours or those members of God's family (almost half the world's population) who survive on less than £4 a day? How many of us are *downtrodden* - perhaps by painful memories or disappointment, guilt or anger over past events, or an unwillingness to forgive others or forgive ourselves.

Jesus tells us that he has been anointed and sent to bring the 'good news', to liberate us. But for this to happen we must first recognize that we are in need of liberating - we too need to be set free.

And of course, Jesus tells us not just to listen to, and receive, the good news but to live it - to *be* the good news for others. By doing this, Jesus' 'mission statement' becomes our mission statement.

....

What is my mission statement? Can I choose to be the 'good news' for others?

22

—

Upside Down

'Thus the last will be first, and the first last.'
(MATTHEW 20:16)

Jesus is unconventional, unorthodox, different. It's no wonder the Jewish authorities hounded him and eventually put him to death. Much of what he said annoyed people. Wisdom can often appear that way - on the surface it makes no sense, especially when it challenges accepted practice, power and authority.

His life has been called the 'Greatest Story Ever Told'. Sometimes his teaching is described as the 'Upside-Down Kingdom'. When you follow him, life is turned upside down. In Jesus' Kingdom those who think they are first will often be last, and those who think they are last will, in God's eyes, often be first. If you want to find your life, you must first lose it. If you want to be great, you must first become a servant. You must love your enemies and do good to those who persecute you. If you want treasure in heaven, you must give all you have to the poor.

Personally, I find all this counterintuitive and if I'm honest, just a little bit crazy, and yet there is something inspiring about a gospel which at first glance seems so far beyond my comprehension and lived experience. In short, it is exactly what one might expect from the Son of God.

Jesus was born in a stable not a palace. He ate at the homes of tax collectors and prostitutes, rather than the rich and famous. He came to call sinners, not the virtuous. He taught that the Sabbath was made for man, not man for the Sabbath. If someone hits you on the cheek, you must offer them the other. If someone asks you for your shirt, give them your coat as well. Jesus is not a conquering hero, but a suffering servant. He writes no best-selling books, commands no armies, wields no political power, is awarded no prizes and does not appear on any Honours List. He shows the world who God is, and is arrested as a blasphemer. He threatens the established order, and after just three years of teaching, is put to death on a cross. The authorities thought they had killed the Jesus movement, but he rises from the dead, and lives forever.

His life is incendiary. He lights a fire in his followers that will lead them to throw caution to the wind and create a church which now has billions of members. To follow Jesus is a radical experience; he is an adventurer who turns lives upside down.

Am I ready for the adventure?

23

Eureka!

'Stand up,' he said 'do not be afraid.'
(Matthew 17:8)

Have you ever had an 'Aha! moment' - a time when you suddenly realised something that you previously didn't comprehend, or perhaps when your understanding of something suddenly changed or clicked? The Greek scientist, Archimedes, is alleged to have experienced a great moment of insight whilst sitting in his bath, which led to him running down the street, naked, shouting Eureka! (I have found it!)

Maybe you have experienced a moment when something has dawned on you, when the penny has dropped: perhaps a person you hadn't previously had much time for has suddenly done something which is thoughtful or compassionate, and your view of them has changed - you see them in a new light, you see their true colours.

During what is known as the transfiguration Jesus leads his most trusted disciples, Peter, James and John up a high mountain so they could be alone. Matthew then records that Jesus 'was transfigured: his face shone like the sun and his clothes became as white as light'. Moses and Elijah appeared and spoke with Jesus. Peter, perhaps overwhelmed and lost for words, can only say 'it is wonderful for us to be here'. 'A bright cloud' then covered them, and from the cloud there came a voice which said, 'This is my Son, the Beloved; he enjoys my favour. Listen to him!'

This must have been a 'Eureka moment' for the disciples - they saw Jesus revealed in all his divine glory. If they were still unsure who Jesus was then this would have removed any doubt from their minds. Something that had previously been somewhat hidden was revealed in all its fullness.

Matthew goes on to say that the disciples were overcome with fear and fell onto the floor, 'But Jesus came up and touched them. 'Stand-up', he said 'do not be afraid.' The response Jesus requires from his followers is one of action. Don't be afraid, get up off your knees. Whenever we are afraid in life, these are the words we need to hear. This is the transfiguration of Peter, James and John. Jesus didn't change who he was on the mountain top, it was the disciples who changed, who had their eyes opened. Perhaps they could now see Jesus everywhere.

All of us are capable of transfiguration. When the egocentric-self dies, then the bright light of Christ, which has always been there, can shine through, and if you look carefully, you can see this light in others.

When we walk this journey with Jesus we don't have to pretend anymore. We get to drop our guard; drop the masks we wear to get us through each day. We don't have to prove to anyone how good or amazing or superior we are. With Christ we leave our egos behind, we have nothing to prove, no point to make, no-one to victimise or exclude, no-one to look down on. Accepted and loved, there is no need to not accept and not love others. Walking with Christ means pretence can disappear, we can be ourselves, we can be *transformed* by his presence.

We can become fully present in the world, and fully present in the service of others - set free to love and to be loved.

....

Is it time for me to stand up and not be afraid?

24

—

It's all about trust

'Do not be afraid, only have faith and she will
be saved'.
(LUKE 8:50-51)

Luke tells us about the daughter of Jairus, a synagogue official who begs Jesus to come and help his twelve-year-old daughter who is dying. Someone then arrives and says not to 'trouble the Master any further' - it's too late, the girl is dead. Jesus then speaks these words to Jairus, 'Do not fear, only believe, and she will be saved'. In some New Testament translations this is written 'only have faith' instead of 'only believe'. 'Faith' and 'belief' in Greek (*pistis*) are used interchangeably, but in English we understand these two words very differently. *Belief* is a word associated with the intellect, with thinking. So we might say 'I believe the world is round, not flat', or 'I believe that global warming is caused by human activity'. Belief describes what we think. So we can also say 'I believe in God' or 'I think God exists'.

With Jairus however, Jesus is not saying 'believe in God and your daughter will be saved', that is, 'give intellectual assent to the proposition that God exists and I will cure her'. What Jesus is saying is, 'have faith, trust me'. This is an appeal to the heart not the head. Jesus isn't saying believe this or that, he is saying trust me, trust God, all will be well. It's not about believing in *something*, but trusting *someone*. Jesus is saying in effect, 'trust me, I won't let you down'. This is one of the most important messages of the entire Gospel.

Trusting of course is much more difficult to do than believing. It's easy to believe stuff, but trust involves courage and commitment. It's easy to say, 'I believe in God', but saying 'I trust in God' demands personal sacrifice and risk. The rich young man in the gospel certainly believed in God, and Mark tells us that he had kept all the commandments since he was young. But he couldn't trust God enough to give his great wealth to the poor and follow the path of Jesus. Believing in God just isn't enough. The theologian Peter Enns suggests that the word *believe* 'should be stricken from all of our Bibles and replaced with *trust*'. 'Believe' involves talking the talk, 'trust' involves walking the walk.

The Christian faith isn't about getting all our beliefs lined up correctly or memorising the catechism. Jesus tells us it's about trusting God and then letting that trust affect the way we treat others.

....

Can placing all my trust in God become my daily habit?

25

—

Mess

'I did not come to call the virtuous,
but sinners.'
(MARK 2:17)

In the early part of the 20th century the phenomenon of 'Messy Church' took root in Britain and has since spread throughout the globe. It's primarily for people who don't already go to church. Meetings aren't necessarily in a church, aren't necessarily on a Sunday, and often involve the children in messy activities and games. Services are family friendly, and everyone and anyone is welcome.

When parents are bringing up their children they are often concerned that their offspring have good friends and role models, that they are 'mixing with the right people'. They might run the slide rule over their children's friends to make sure that none of them are 'a bad influence'. One day they might hope their children will settle down, get a good job, make a home for themselves, fall in love, and perhaps get married and have children, so that they might become grandparents.

Perhaps Mary and Joseph had the same hopes for Jesus when he was growing up? If so, they were to be disappointed. By many standards his life and subsequent painful death on the cross was a disaster. Jesus did not mix in the right circles.

DOING CHRISTIANITY

He shunned the wealthy and influential, and poured scorn on the accepted religious leaders of the day. He was penniless and largely homeless, as he wandered from place to place preaching the gospel. The company he kept 'left a lot to be desired'. To the dismay of many he welcomed tax collectors and prostitutes, he was happy talking to foreigners and women, and he reached out to the sick and the leper. He said he had come for the sinner rather than the virtuous, and he urged his followers to visit those in prison and care for the lowly. Even when he is dying on the cross, he reaches out to the convicted thief who is crucified at his side, telling him he will be with him in paradise.

When men want to change the course of history they send for the generals and politicians - Jesus on the other hand calls up the meek, the hungry, the mourners and the peacemakers.

Jesus came for the marginalised, the dispossessed and excluded; he sought out 'life's losers' not the fortunate few or those who think they have 'made it'. He showed us that God is at home in the everyday messiness of life. We love everything to be ordered and 'just so', but Jesus thrived in the unconventional and unorthodox.

Don't worry if your life is messy, don't worry if your life isn't perfect, don't worry if you are anxious or afraid, excluded or marginalised. Know that God thrives in the messiness and imperfection of life; he is constantly trying to get our attention, to help us see the potential for goodness we all possess. And by concealing holiness in the mess of life he ensures that only the humble can find it.

Most of us don't have 'perfect lives', just varying degrees of messiness. But the Good News is - that is precisely where you will find Christ waiting for us.

....

Can I see Christ in the mess?

26

—

Simon the Pharisee

*'Simon,' he said 'you see this woman? I came
into your house, and you poured no water over
my feet, but she has poured out her tears over
my feet and wiped them away with her hair.
You gave me no kiss, but she has been covering
my feet with kisses ever since I came in... For
this reason I tell you that her sins, her many
sins, must have been forgiven her, or she would
not have shown such great love. It is the man
who is forgiven little who shows little love.'*
(LUKE 7:44-48)

In the TV comedy 'Keeping Up Appearances' the central
character, Hyacinth Bucket (pronounced 'Bouquet') is a
snobbish social climber who is constantly trying to prove
her superiority, looking down on the habits and ideas of those
whom she considers are lower than her. She takes every opportunity to impress her neighbours with her perceived re-
finement and polish. We find it amusing partly because we
can see ourselves in Hyacinth, in those moments when we
are quick to judge others, to boast about our achievements
and demonstrate how marvellous we are!

DOING CHRISTIANITY

Simon the Pharisee asks Jesus to his house for a meal. A woman 'who had a bad name in the town' enters and begins to bathe Jesus' feet with her tears. Interestingly Jesus is not in the least embarrassed or disturbed by this - he is not worried about what others may think. Simon on the other hand, is scandalized that Jesus is allowing a sinner to touch him in this way.

Jesus sees through Simon's outward appearance to his judgmental and dismissive inner self. He sees how Simon pays lip service to politeness yet has a heart of stone. The woman meanwhile, for all her bad reputation, is aware of her need of God's grace and forgiveness. She knows she has much that needs to be forgiven, and she is exuberantly grateful that God has forgiven her sins and set her free. Her outpouring of love and generosity for Jesus is a measure of how far she has come, of her inner transformation. Her past is irrelevant, what matters now is not her reputation, but her present and future. She is forgiven, and ready to relate to God and neighbour in a new way.

Simon meanwhile has had no such change; he is set in his ways, he is comfortable with his life and position, quite happy with 'things as they are', quick to judge, unwilling to accept any views which depart from his own legalistic mindset. He is oblivious to his own sin, and his own desperate need of God.

Luke does not tell us what happens to Simon the Pharisee. Did this encounter lead him to accept that he too was a sinner, that he too needed to be transformed, to let his guard down, to reach out in faith to the God of mercy and compassion?

His time has come and gone; we will never know the choice that Simon made. We, however, do still have time to make our own choice about the kind of person we want to be...

....

Am I so concerned with keeping up outward appearances
that I fail to see the need for inner transformation?

27

—

An Example

'I have given you an example so that you may
copy what I have done to you.'
(JOHN 13:15)

There was controversy in the Catholic Church a few years ago when some of the words of the Mass were changed. In the Eucharistic prayer the word 'cup' was replaced with 'chalice', and the prayer 'Lord I am not worthy to receive you' was changed to 'Lord I am not worthy that you should enter under my roof'. Some worshippers were outraged with the changes and there were angry letters of complaint in the Catholic press. Words matter. We live in a world of words. I have heard thousands of words in sermons and homilies preached from the pulpit. Think of all the books written about religion and theology. Billions of words. Words are important of course, but let's take a step back... they are just words after all.

Jesus spent three years teaching and preaching, and a tiny fraction of his words are recorded in the four gospels. Most of what he said was never written down. Yet Jesus didn't just preach - he backed up all his words with actions. We understand a huge amount from what he said, but we learn just as much, if not more, from what he did.

He didn't just tell people he was the Bread of Life; he fed the five thousand who came to listen to him. Rather than just telling people he would set them free, he cured them of their blindness and let the paralyzed walk again. He said he could forgive sins, and then rescued the sinner from being stoned by an angry mob. He said he was 'the Life', and then raised his friend Lazarus from the dead. Instead of just telling his disciples to serve others, he gets down on his knees and washes their feet.

He didn't just ask people to change using fine words, he showed them 'the Way', and he enables us to see how we can live differently. Instead of just speaking about 'living life to the full', he gives his listeners a roadmap, an example to follow. He spoke about the dangers of money and possessions, then lived without a purse or a haversack. He told his disciples to forgive, then spent his days forgiving the sins of those who came to him. Instead of just teaching his followers how to pray, he took every opportunity he could to withdraw from the crowds and speak to his Father. He talks about the Gospel of Love, then offers himself on the cross to show how much he loves us - he tells his followers to take up their cross, and then carries his own cross to Calvary. He says that he is the 'Resurrection and the Life', and then rises from the dead to show us the way to live.

Jesus guides us not just by his teachings, but by the manner in which he conducts himself, *by the things he does*. Jesus in effect says to us: 'you will know them by their fruits, and my fruits are gentleness, kindness, patience and tolerance'. In his dealings with those who crowd around him searching for answers he is listening, healing and forgiving. He speaks truth to power, he tells it like it is, but always with compassion and understanding. We all learn by doing, and by watching others doing, and to watch Jesus is to watch the man who walked the same path that we walk now, with all the suffering, temptation and disappointment that we too endure. We learn from Jesus' teachings of course, but when we watch him in action we can fall in love with him, just as the disciples did.

And that relationship is central to the Christian experience. We don't just hear the words of Jesus and try to follow his example in our dealings with others, we enter into relationship with him. We acknowledge his presence in us, and his love for us, and this connection not only gives us a sense of security and divine fellowship but impels us to reach out in love to the rest of God's creation.

Jesus says he is 'The Way', but this way does not consist of believing in certain things about Jesus. We aren't converted to new life by an intellectual decision to believe that 'Jesus is Lord'. That would be absurd, what Marcus Borg describes as 'salvation by syllables'. The way of Jesus is the path of personal change, of dying (to self) and resurrection - a way he embodies and incarnates in his own life. He has gone before us to show us how it's done, to reveal what a spirit-filled human life looks like. He tells us in words that he is Way, the Truth and the Life – and then shows us how to live the Way, the Truth and the Life.

. . . .

Spend some time today reading the Gospel and notice not just what Jesus says but how he says it - watch how he behaves, the way he talks to people, how he responds to those in need.

28

—

The Rich Young Man

'There is one thing you lack, go and sell everything you own and give the money to the poor, and you will have treasure in heaven; then come, follow me.'
(MARK 10:21)

When I was a teacher I used to ask my sixth form students what they would do if they won ten million pounds on the lottery. Their answers were always the same. They would buy an apartment, a car, some new designer clothes and go on exotic holidays. Some even suggested they would give up college and university saying, 'what would be the point of continuing?' Carefully invested they would be 'set up for life' financially - no need to acquire school qualifications or a degree or even necessarily get a job. They all commented on what a stroke of good fortune it would be. There was never any question about whether getting all this money would be a good thing, whether it would make them happy or not, and no-one ever said they would refuse the cash, or give it all to charity! The lesson would then continue with me reading this story from Mark's gospel.

I have always felt sorry for the rich young man - perhaps we can all see something of ourselves in him? When he asks what he needs to do to 'inherit eternal life' Jesus says, 'keep the Commandments'. The man says, yes I have kept these, what more do I need to do? Jesus then tells him to 'go and sell everything you own and give the money to the poor', but the man goes away sad because 'he was a man of great wealth'. He has yet to learn the truth that we grow spiritually by reducing our material possessions. He hasn't understood that less is more in the kingdom of heaven. There is no doubt that this is a tough ask; it's not just 'give something to charity', it's give everything away, and 'follow me'.

Jesus could see that the rich young man felt entitled – maybe the man thought he had worked hard, so 'deserved' to be wealthy? However, he was trapped by what he owned, he needed nothing, so in the end he gets nothing spiritually. Jesus asks him to become a kind of 'beggar', to lose his sense of entitlement and become dependent on God alone.

Jesus believes that we can end up worshipping money - 'No one can be the slave of two masters ... you cannot be the slave both of God and of money'. (Matthew 6:24). He teaches that, 'where your treasure is, there will your heart be also' (Luke 12:34), and he wants our hearts to be free to love God and neighbour. But as a society we have become obsessed with money, there is even a term - affluenza - used to describe the sickness of excessive wealth-seeking in a modern consumerist age. For many of us acquiring as much money and possessions as possible has become an addiction, an unhealthy preoccupation, and for some their whole life's work. It was a Trappist monk, Thomas Merton, who pointed out that we can spend our whole life climbing the 'ladder of success', only to find, once we reach the top, that the ladder is leaning against the wrong wall.

If life is so concerned with grabbing, counting and holding onto money and possessions, then our hands are not free to bless or to receive. Money will buy you a car, but it is a temporary gain - one day that car will end up on the scrap-heap. Investing in our relationships however is a permanent win for us, because love is never wasted.

Soren Kierkegaard said: 'The Bible is very easy to understand. But we Christians ... pretend to be unable to understand it because we know very well that the minute we understand it, we are obliged to act accordingly'. The rich young man felt uncomfortable on hearing the words of Jesus, and they are difficult verses for us too. Compared with most people on the planet those of us who live in the West are generally people of 'great wealth'. We rarely go hungry or thirsty, most of us have a roof over our heads, a TV, a phone, a washing machine, and dozens of possessions. The words of Jesus are supposed to challenge the rich young man, and us, out of complacency. Money can be a blessing or a curse; it can be used to help others or to help ourselves.

St. Francis of Assisi did exactly as Jesus instructed - he was a wealthy young man, yet he gave all this up and devoted the rest of his life to helping the poor. He understood that money can't buy happiness or peace of mind.

Finally, Mark's Gospel tells us that just before Jesus asked the man to sell everything, he 'looked steadily at him and loved him'. However we choose to respond to Jesus' teaching, we can be sure that his steady gaze of love will always fall on us. Although the rich young man went away sad, we will never know whether he later reflected on all that he had heard, and in the fullness of time, and by the grace of God, perhaps put aside his wealth and followed Jesus. The Gospel doesn't tell us, but I hope he did.

....

What would I do with a lottery win?

29

—

I am always with you

*'And know that I am with you always; yes, to
the end of time.'*
(MATTHEW 28:20)

Much of what we experience in life is fleeting – it comes and goes. Our childhood, our schooling, our working life, our health, and of course our looks! So many things are transient – even our relationships. Many people come in and out of our lives, some of them very dear to us. We may even find that God comes in and out of our life, in the sense that sometimes we might feel close to him and at other times very distant. We may even go through periods when we stop believing altogether.

Many people have spoken about an epidemic of loneliness in the modern world, especially in older generations. What is striking however is that in the UK, the Office for National Statistics reported that the 16-24 age group were three times more likely than those over 65 to say they 'often or always' felt lonely. In an age of supposed connectivity many feel isolated and cut off, in fact surveys have suggested that as people increase their use of social media, they report feeling *more* not less lonely.

DOING CHRISTIANITY

Jesus tells us that whatever happens he is always there for us. Even when we stop believing in him, he never stops believing in us. Even when we feel alone, he is by our side - we need never experience loneliness again.

God loved us so much that he became one of us in Jesus, and promises to be with us always, whoever we are, and whatever we have done. The love of God and the presence of Christ is not a transient, fleeting thing, and it does not depend on our goodness or faithfulness. It is constant and lasts forever.

....

Stop and take a moment to experience the presence of God in the here and now.

30
—
Just a good story?

'The reason I talk to them in parables is that they look without seeing and listen without hearing or understanding. So in their case this prophecy of Isaiah is being fulfilled: You will listen and listen again, but not understand, see and see again, but not perceive. For the heart of this nation has grown coarse, their ears are dull of hearing, and they have shut their eyes, for fear they should see with their eyes, hear with their ears, understand with their heart, and be converted and be healed by me.'
(MATTHEW 13:13-15)

When I was training to be a teacher we were told that it was not our role to do all the work in the classroom, to spoon-feed our students - we had to make them do most of the work. If a student can grasp an idea themselves, can make the connections and internalise the learning, then that knowledge or concept is more likely to be remembered and applied. Hence Jesus, the master teacher, often speaks in parables, which make up a third of the gospels of Matthew, Mark and Luke. Stories about robbery, lost sheep, lost sons and wedding feasts. Stories about things that never took place, but actually take place all the time - in every town and city, on every continent, on every day, in every year of human existence. Interestingly, Jesus rarely mentions *God* in the parables; they are not 'other-worldly' stories but focus on the ordinary events of this world now.

He knows such stories will stay long in the minds of those who hear them; he hopes that they will make the connections, that the penny will drop, and they will begin to see life from a fresh perspective. Churches often create catechisms, with all the answers. Jesus on the other hand often just asks questions, creating problems for his listeners to grapple with rather than spoon-feeding them solutions. It's the grappling that leads to spiritual growth.

The fact that so many people today can remember the parables is a testament to Jesus' teaching power. Almost everyone has heard the parable of the Good Samaritan and they are usually impressed: 'What a lovely story, how heart-warming!'

But the parables are designed to go deeper than this. The gospel writers did not record them so that future readers could admire their prose or marvel over Jesus' undoubted skills as a storyteller. They were not interested in winning a prize for 'best short story'. The whole point of a parable is to help us to discover for ourselves something profound, to precipitate a 'light bulb moment' which will inspire us to transform our behaviour and become a different person. To say: 'In future I will not ignore that person who needs help, I will copy this Samaritan in the way I respond to the needy'.

If there is no change in us then the world isn't changed; the parable just lives on in the pages of the Bible - nothing happens, the book is closed, there is a brief moment of admiration perhaps, and then life moves on. But Jesus wants more from us - his desire for his followers is to: 'understand with their heart, and be converted and be healed by me'. The incarnation means 'the word became flesh' and Jesus wants the parable to become a lived reality, to become 'enfleshed' in our world, to leap out from the page and into our lives.

....

Take time to read some of the parables again and see how you can make them come alive in your own life.

31

We tried to stop him

*John said to him, 'Master, we saw a man
who is not one of us casting out devils in your
name; and because he was not one of us we
tried to stop him'. But Jesus said, 'You must
not stop him: no one who works a miracle in
my name is likely to speak evil of me. Anyone
who is not against us is for us.'*
(MARK 9:38-40)

Humans are tribal, often wishing to stick with their own group, mixing with people like themselves and often looking down on those they see as different. Politics of course is all about tribalism - Margaret Thatcher once famously asked her colleagues if a fellow politician was 'one of us'. The implication being that if you are not 'one of us' you are 'one of them' - an obstacle, an opponent, an enemy.

Jesus had no time for this kind of posturing. The disciples complain about trying to stop a man casting out demons in the name of Jesus. They tell Jesus that he is not 'one of us', not part of our little group - perhaps they are jealous of their own status and power as part of Jesus' inner circle? How dare anyone else claim to be speaking in Jesus' name! But there is no copyright on the Holy Spirit; Jesus is not a brand that needs to be protected by patent. It is not the case that the disciples are the 'chosen few' and only they have the power to help the needy. Jesus is no doubt delighted that goodness is spreading, his message is going viral, the Spirit is blowing where it wills. 'You must not stop him' he says. Unlike most of us, he assumes that if someone is not against him, then they are *for him*. And why would that not be the case - Jesus is an optimist, he always sees the good in others, he always sees God in others.

As a teacher I can remember my own faith being enhanced by my Hindu and Muslim students. John Wesley spoke out against that 'miserable bigotry that makes many so unready to believe that there is any work of God but among themselves'. The Spirit of God is within us all, empowering us whatever our faith, or lack of it, whether we are conscious of it or not. The Swiss psychoanalyst Carl Jung had the following words inscribed above his doorway (and on his gravestone): 'Summoned or not, God will be there'.

Wherever love exists, whenever a person is helped by another, then God is there, whether that helper is a Christian, someone of another faith, someone of no faith or a committed atheist. The loving is the important thing, not the label we attach to someone. Acts of love are a clear sign of the Holy Spirit at work and should strengthen rather than diminish our faith. God's grace is for everyone and isn't bound by our human small mindedness or prejudice.

Does it matter to the hungry child in Africa if the food she receives comes from the Red Cross or the Red Crescent? Jesus tells us that it's the action that matters - the man the disciples were complaining about was doing good, helping those in distress. Jesus seems to be saying to the disciples:

'Get over yourselves, this isn't about you, or our little clique, God is so much bigger and more generous than you can imagine'.

....

How do I view those who aren't in my group?

32

—

What about you?

Then Jesus said to the Twelve, 'What about you, do you want to go away too? Simon Peter answered, 'Lord, who shall we go to? You have the message of eternal life, and we believe; we know that you are the Holy One of God.'
(JOHN 6:67-69)

Have you ever 'walked away' from Christ? The teachings of Jesus are challenging and there are aspects which are hard to believe. Many of those who knew Jesus, listened to his teaching and then walked away, having decided that they couldn't follow him. This prompted Jesus to pose the question above.

If those who actually met Jesus left him, then it is not surprising that those of us who have 'not seen' have times when we 'walk away' from Jesus.

The decision to follow Christ is less a one-off event, more an on-going commitment to follow his example and live out his teachings in our daily lives. Although Peter doesn't understand everything about Jesus, he does recognise that if he leaves him, then 'Lord, who shall we go to?' He can see that there are other pathways he can follow, but he recognises that Jesus offers the 'gifts of spirit and life', things the world cannot give. All of us know, deep down, that the material things of this world can never truly satisfy the deepest longings of our heart. Peter is starting to see the world as Jesus sees it, and in the process is finding that his rather humdrum, routine life is becoming something filled with hope and promise. The Gospel has the potential to transform the ordinary into something beautiful; Peter understands that there is really nowhere else to go.

We too can either follow the crowd or listen to that inner voice gently calling us to follow Christ.

....

Have you ever 'walked away' from Jesus?

33

—

I Am

'I tell you most solemnly, before Abraham
ever was, I Am'.
(JOHN 8:58)

In Exodus 3 we read that God appeared to Moses in 'the shape of a flame of fire coming from the middle of a bush'. Moses approaches the burning bush and asks God what name he should give to the Israelites if they ask him who he has been talking to, 'And God said to Moses, I Am who I Am.'

God is he who is ever-present, never changing and eternal. He is the beginning and the end, the one who is, who was and who is to come - the Almighty. No matter what words we use, what language we employ, we can never hope to even begin to explain the fullness of God. He is simply the great 'I Am'.

In the Gospel Jesus refers to himself as the 'I Am'. On one occasion Jesus mentions Abraham in his teaching, and some of his listeners question him scornfully saying, 'You are not fifty yet, and you have seen Abraham!' Jesus replies, 'before Abraham ever was, I Am'. Recognising the significance of what he had said, the Jews get ready to stone him for blasphemy, but Jesus hides and slips away.

There have been many great saints and holy men and women throughout history, but none have used the 'I am' statement. Great saints such as St Francis or Mother Teresa always pointed away from themselves, they made no claims on their own behalf, urging us to simply fix our gaze on God.

Jesus is different. John records him making seven references to himself as 'I Am': 'I am the bread of life'; 'I am the light of the world'; 'I am the gate'; 'I am the Good Shepherd'; 'I am the resurrection and the life'; 'I am the way, the truth and the life'; 'I am the true vine'. These statements summarise Jesus' mission. He has come to feed us, to provide light for our journey, he is the gate through which we must pass on the road of life. He is the shepherd who will bring us home and lead us to our own resurrection. He is the true vine, and because we are connected to him and abide in him, we can bear fruit that will last.

With these statements Jesus does not leave his listeners in any doubt as to who he was claiming to be; ultimately these claims were to lead to his arrest and execution for blasphemy.

If the universe has existed for nearly 14 billion years, then God's serious involvement could not begin a mere two thousand years ago with the birth of Jesus. As Richard Rohr argues in his book 'The Universal Christ', the Spirit of Christ is not the same as the person of Jesus. Christ is not just Jesus' last name. The *'Cosmic Christ'*, that is the love of God, has been around since time began and is part of all creation and exists in all peoples. *The historical Jesus* incarnates that spirit, that love of God, for everyone and everything. It is Jesus we relate to and fall in love with. Whilst Jesus is, for me, the best way to access the Spirit of God this does not mean that God cannot be accessed through other religions or ways of being. The universal Christ, incarnate in time in Jesus, is still being revealed to us, and this revelation will continue till the end. Theologians like Marcus Borg highlight the distinction between the flesh and blood pre-Easter Jesus, and the post-Easter Christ. After the Resurrection it is the Universal Christ who appears to the disciples, the Christ we still experience today.

Christ, the eternal 'I Am', was there at the beginning of creation (the first incarnation) and will be there at the end – the Alpha and the Omega. John tells us in the prologue to his gospel: 'In the beginning was the Word: the Word was with God and the word was God. He was with God in the beginning. Through him all things came to be, not one thing had its being but through him. All that came to be had life in him and that life was the light of men, a light that shines in the dark...'

Christ is the 'Word'. Unlike the other three gospel writers, John begins his story before the beginning of time, showing us that Christ has always been: he was there at the start, a creative power in the universe and a light shining in the dark. In Jesus, the eternal Christ is made flesh and now lives among us. Heaven and earth meet in the incarnation - the eternal has come to us - bringing light into our darkness. Hence Jesus was able to say, 'I am the Light of the world', a Light that was there at the very beginning. Jesus doesn't just reveal the word of God to humanity - he is the Word.

And above all else, the Word is Love. That is the first and the last word. Love ushers all of us into the world, and in the fullness of time ushers us out. This Word is the creative heartbeat of the cosmos. John starts his gospel with his central message - 'the Word was God', and ends much later with the same proclamation, as doubting Thomas exclaims to Jesus, 'My Lord and my God!'

In John's first letter he writes: 'Something which has existed since the beginning, that we have heard, and we have seen with our own eyes; that we have watched and touched with our hands: the Word, who is life - this is our subject'.

And the eternal Christ is with us today, always in the present, always available. As the author of Hebrews 13:8-9 puts it, 'Jesus Christ is the same today as he was yesterday and as he will be forever.'

....

Can I recognise Christ as the 'I Am', always present, in the here and now of my life?

If you've never read John's Gospel from beginning to end (from the Prologue to the Risen Lord) then I urge you to do so. It doesn't take long and it's an extraordinary piece of writing (quite different from the other three gospels).

34
—

Becoming like little children

So he called a little child to him and set the
child in front of them. Then he said, 'I tell
you solemnly, unless you change and become
like little children you will never enter the
kingdom of heaven.'
(MATTHEW 18:2-4)

Jesus wants us to become like little children. In what way? A child is trusting, and one of the major themes of this book is that we need to place our trust in God – in Him all will be well. A child has an acceptance and an honesty that is often missing in adults, where cynicism and world weariness have made us suspicious and judgmental. A child is not afraid to ask when they need something; and children are not afraid or ashamed to show their emotions. It is easy to make a child smile - they are open to joy and easy laughter in a way adults have often long forgotten. They are not afraid to make a fool of themselves from time to time, and they have not yet learnt to discriminate against others who are different. They don't have any complicated theological beliefs.

A small child's needs are simple. They don't yet understand the attraction of coins and banknotes, they aren't worried about career or status, they aren't too bothered about combing their hair or tucking their shirt in before they go outside! Open to learning new things they seek out enjoyment wherever they can, and they often stand in awe and wonder at new and exciting events and experiences - they have not yet become jaded by the new. They seek out friends and ways of cooperating with them in play. They are often quite happy to simply be in the present moment, going with the flow, playing 'hide and seek' or crayoning a picture.

Children need a home, food, drink and warmth, and we too need a spiritual home, somewhere to be fed the Bread of life, drink the water that will permanently quench our thirst and rest in the warmth of the light of God. Children know they can't do everything on their own - without parents and others they wouldn't survive. Above all else children have a deep need to be loved - they bond with significant others because somewhere deep down they know they have to, in order to flourish. Their vulnerability is a doorway to love.

Jesus is not saying we must infantilize ourselves. We have an adult brain and we need to use it, but as we age, we do have a choice. We can become cynical, world-weary, suspicious of everyone we meet, viewing the world as a hostile, unfriendly place, seeing God as a distant, judgmental figure. Or we can become like a child - placing trust in our heavenly Father, recognising our need of him, and one another, and living accordingly.

What child-like qualities do I need to cultivate?

35

—

When the storm comes

Then it began to blow a gale and the waves
were breaking into the boat so that it was
almost swamped. But he was in the stern, his
head on the cushion, asleep.
(MARK 4:37-39)

Our lives are like the weather. Some days the sun shines all day and all is well. At other times it just never seems to stop raining, and there are moments in life when the most terrible storms arrive, often without warning, perhaps threatening our very existence, or affecting our physical or mental well-being.

Jesus asks his disciples to get in a boat on the Sea of Galilee: 'Let us cross over to the other side.' Of course he wanted to cross the lake, but we can also see it as Jesus saying: 'Let's leave the quiet waters and go to the other side - the side of life which is not so calm, the times of adversity, sickness, and personal hardship where your faith will be tested'.

When they set sail, a great storm comes down and threatens to swamp the boat. The disciples were professional fishermen accustomed to adverse weather at sea, so this storm must have been particularly bad for them to fear for their lives. Jesus is asleep and they wake him: 'Master, do you not care? We are going down!' This is often our reaction too - in the face of personal adversity we often cry out with the disciples, 'God don't you care?'

After Jesus 'rebuked the wind' and quietened the waves Mark tells us that the disciples were 'terrified'. Was this because of the storm I wonder, or were they terrified at the awesome power over nature that Jesus had displayed? 'Who can this be?' they asked themselves, 'Even the wind and the sea obey him.'

Jesus appears to be a little annoyed with the disciples, 'Why are you so frightened?' he says, 'How is it that you have no faith?' Perhaps he would have preferred it if they hadn't woken him up, and just trusted that if he were with them, everything would be fine.

When we experience the storms of life, we may think God is asleep, but his loving care is always with us. Whatever the weather, we can be confident that as St Paul says, 'all things work together for good', we are always held in the palm of God's hand. Like the disciples our faith is weak, but the good news is that it doesn't matter whether we have a strong or a weak faith - Jesus still saves us.

Let the storms of life be our teachers. When the rain subsides, there is often clarity, a freshness in the air, and a different perspective on who we are, and where we are going. When you have come through a storm you are never the same person. Each storm is an opportunity to face your fears, and to place your trust in the God who is never asleep and will never leave you alone when the going gets tough.

....

May I always remember that whatever storms life throws at me, Christ is always in the boat with me and never leaves my side.

36

—

The Cross

and being as all men are, he was humbler yet,
even to accepting death, death on a cross.
(PHILIPPIANS 2:7-8)

The cross, the symbol of the Christian faith, has been the subject of much theological discussion through the ages. In the early church, Origen and others thought that Jesus' death was a ransom sacrifice paid by God to Satan to repay the debt of original sin on human souls. The redemption of Christ was in effect a 'buying back' of our souls, an appeasement for a Father 'offended' by our sin. Anselm refined this idea with the concept of atonement - Christ's death makes amends for and frees us from our sins and reconciles us to the Father. Aquinas later taught that 'Christ bore a satisfactory punishment, not for his, but for our sins.' Hence we can say 'Jesus died for our sins'.

In recent years theologians have begun to look critically at such ideas. This traditional theology casts the Father as rather 'small minded', unable or unwilling to forgive our sins without some sacrifice from his Son. Instead of seeing the saving work of God as happening at all times and everywhere, the atonement sees it as a one-off event, a payment required by a Father who demands some sort of retribution. This idea of a 'punishing Father' can make people fearful of God.

Many theologians now see the crucifixion not as a necessary 'punishment' for our wrongdoing but a supreme act of sacrificial love which highlights the reason Jesus came to us - to heal rather than condemn, to show us the depth of his love, to show us the route from sin to life, from darkness to light. In effect Jesus is saying on the cross, 'look how much I love you'. The cross is a symbol of love not punishment. This love is freely given to us and is not earned by some kind of bargain with the Father. God's healing love and forgiveness is not paid for, it is always free and given abundantly.

By his death on the cross Jesus tells us that our pain is his pain, every act of suffering we experience is also His. Hence we are never alone in our pain, our grief, our death. Jesus does not passively watch our pain and suffering from a distance; he is *in* our suffering, *by* our side, *in* our pain. He is the God of everyone who suffers. And knowing that he suffers with us, and in us, gives us the opportunity to turn suffering into love, pain into hope, death into resurrection. Just as Jesus surrendered to his suffering, at times we too will be called to the cross, called to sacrifice and surrender in love as we experience our own moments of pain and loss. By understanding how love conquers death on the cross, and by uniting our suffering with his, we begin to glimpse the Light of Love in our own pain and darkness.

Jesus, fully man, flesh and blood, suffers on the cross to tell us that whatever we endure, he has endured, he is with us in our pain, and there is a loving liberation and a healing resurrection close at hand. The cross does save us, it does free us from sin, but not perhaps in the way we once thought.

In my moments of pain can I unite my suffering with Christ's on the cross, and together turn loss into love?

37

—

Who do you say I am?

he put this question to his disciples...
'But you ... who do you say I am?'
(Matthew 16:13-16)

Getting feedback is now a part of almost every job appraisal. We all want to know what people think of us and Jesus is no different - he wants to know who people think he is. The disciples tell him that some say he is John the Baptist, Elijah or one of the prophets.

It's a question that Jesus also puts to each of us - 'who do you say I am?'

Step Two has been all about trying to find an answer to the question, 'who is Jesus for you?' Is he a distant historical figure who said some nice things but has little or no relevance to your life and the world of today? Is he a philosophical dreamer who asks you to 'turn the other cheek' or 'give all you have to the poor' - high minded ideas that are impossible to put into practice? Is he just another good man, a holy man, to be studied and admired perhaps? Is he someone to be slightly fearful of - someone who will one day judge us, and perhaps find us wanting? Or someone we consider on a Sunday, but rarely give a thought to for the rest of the week?

Peter's reply is: 'You are the Christ, the Son of the living God'. God in human form, the Word made flesh. Jesus responds by saying that Peter is 'a happy man!', and he goes on to state that Peter is the rock on which the future Church will be built. Peter's faith-filled answer to the question has both confirmed his personal discipleship, and opened the door to the birth of the Church. Our answer to Jesus' question will have consequences for us too.

How do I respond to the question 'Who do you say I am', and what are the consequences for me which might flow from my answer?

STEP THREE

Who am I?

I learnt a lot about myself when I met my first atheist at the age of eighteen. I'd had an orthodox Catholic upbringing, spending thirteen years in Church schools, attending Mass every Sunday, and all my family and friends were Christian. I didn't expect to make friends with an atheist, yet here was someone who was kind, thoughtful, generous, inclusive, non-judgemental, and quick to forgive and forget. The thought struck me that here was someone who 'practised' Christianity far better than I did - not by believing in certain things but by simply being a good person. I learnt that being a Christian was about doing not believing - orthopraxis rather than orthodoxy.

In the gospels Jesus asks us to change our behaviour, to transform ourselves. But before we can see and do things differently we need to understand who we are. A story about St Francis of Assisi relates how a brother was watching Francis in prayer and heard him say, 'Who are you, Lord my God, and who am I?'

In Step 3 we focus on 'Who am I?' and in the passages that follow Jesus encourages us to put aside our worries, to trust him in all things and live in the present moment. We will learn how to recognise and let go of our ego-driven-self in order to see ourselves as God sees us, and understand the truth that Christ 'lives in me, and I in him.'

As Richard Rohr has said, "When you get your, 'Who am I?', question right, your, 'What should I do?' questions tend to take care of themselves."

38

—

God's work of art

We are God's work of art, created in
Christ Jesus to live the good life as from the
beginning he had meant us to live it.
(EPHESIANS 2:10)

TV shows like the X Factor seem to delight in putting
before the judges a small number of singers who are
convinced they are the next Frank Sinatra but can
hardly sing a note. They have a rather inflated opinion of
themselves and their singing prowess but are eventually told
the harsh truth by the panel of judges.

The reality is, however, that many people today do not
think enough of themselves. Young people in particular often
feel that they are not listened to, that they don't matter. We
sometimes feel as if we are defined by what people say about
us, especially if those comments are negative. Jesus teaches
us that in God's eyes everyone matters, no one is more important than anybody else, and we all have a part to play in
the task of creating the kingdom of heaven. Each of us has a
journey to take, and a role to play, which no one else can do.

Sadly, society often treats us like objects rather than children of God. Education tends to stress the importance of
exam results above all else. Workers can be exploited, paid

poorly for the work they do, and treated as commodities. Women and minorities are often treated as second-class citizens. Those with disabilities are frequently side-lined or neglected. The criminal justice system 'writes off' thousands of people each year. At the end of life the elderly are often robbed of their dignity and value and pushed to one side. And the world tends to prize good looks, wealth and intelligence above character and integrity.

It can appear that we are hamsters on a wheel, endlessly striving, running fast - and going nowhere. We are sold false dreams about happiness, and told the lie that if we consume more, own more, buy more, we will *be* more. We are told that success is measured by what we have, rather than who we are. And of course, if we can't value ourselves, then it's hard to value others.

This is Bad News not the Good News. Jesus tells us that our value is not monetary, our worth is not in what we own, our dignity does not consist in worldly glamour or fame. We cannot be valued more highly - we are loved unconditionally by God, and that will never change. God doesn't define us by our mistakes or mis-steps, or by what others may think of us. We will never be more loved by God, no matter how many exam certificates we acquire, promotions at work we achieve, or awards we are given.

Our destiny is to seek and discover the truth about ourselves - who we are, and what we were created for: 'Before I formed you in the womb I knew you; before you came to birth I consecrated you' (Jeremiah 1:5). Jesus came to tell us that we are God's work of art, his masterpiece, consecrated and made holy before we were born. When we realise this, then our journey to wholeness can begin.

Can I see myself as God's work of art?

39

—

You are my beloved

And a voice spoke from heaven, 'This is my Son, the Beloved; my favour rests on him'.
(MATTHEW 3:17)

'And did you get what you wanted from this life...' That is the question that Raymond Carver asks in his poem 'Late Fragment' published just before he died at the age of fifty. We can only answer this question if we know who we are.

God is more concerned with who we are than what we believe. But who am I exactly? We often define ourselves by our status or occupation: I'm an accountant, a shop assistant, a pensioner. Or perhaps by what we have: I'm a home-owner, a British passport holder, I'm someone with a BMW!

When Jesus is baptised by John the Baptist in the river Jordan, he hears a voice saying: 'This is my Son, the Beloved; my favour rests on him'. Jesus came to let us know that we are as beloved as he is. This is who I am.

This is perhaps the most important message of the Gospel. God is our first love. He knitted us together in our mother's womb, he has written our name in the palm of his hand. God says - you belong to me, you are my beloved. This 'beloved-ness' does not depend on our occupation or our status.

Nor does it depend on how 'good' we are, or how sinful we have been. It is not restricted to a particular ethnic group, religion, gender or sexual orientation. It is not restricted to believers. It is just how God sees us - all of us. In the words of St Augustine, 'God loves each of us as if there were only one of us.'

What a difference it would make to us if we could only have the imagination to see ourselves as God sees us. When we are loved by another we feel amazing, unique, safe, joyful and held secure. This is how God wants us to feel all of the time.

We too must listen to the voice that Jesus heard by the river Jordan. The voice that calls us 'beloved'. Hold on to this truth when life is going well but also when the weight of the world is on your shoulders, when your faith is strong and when your faith is shaky, when you feel successful and happy and when you feel upset or alone. And knowing that God loves us, just as we are, will give us the confidence to reach out to love others, which is the whole point of everything.

....

Raymond Carver answers his question at the end of his poem – he got what he wanted from life: 'To call myself beloved, to feel myself beloved on the earth'.

What difference would it make to my life if I could see myself as God's beloved son or daughter? Consider for a while St Paul's words: 'neither death nor life...nothing that exists, nothing still to come, not any power, nor any created thing, can ever come between us and the love of God made visible in Christ Jesus our Lord'. (Romans 8:38-39)

40
—
This might cheer you up!

*The Spirit too comes to help us in
our weakness.*
(ROMANS 8:26)

Some years ago I wrote a couple of school textbooks. It wasn't easy. In order to meet the publisher's deadlines I had to write a page a day. However, each morning I would re-read the previous day's work, decide I wasn't happy with the page I had written and begin all over again. Consequently, I was getting nowhere fast - my desire to write the 'perfect textbook' was preventing me from writing anything. So I made myself a big sign which read 'It doesn't have to be perfect' and stuck it over my desk. I decided not to rewrite anything - if it was 'good enough' then it would be OK, and 'it doesn't have to be perfect' happily became my life mantra! (the downside to this is several mediocre DIY jobs around the house).

Our journey through life is often beset with failure and weariness. Surrounded as we are with seeming perfection on TV and social media we can often find ourselves disappointed that our lives have not turned out 'perfectly'. We tend to see everything as a competition: who can earn the most, buy the biggest house, be most popular, have the most 'likes' on our social media posts, be the most 'successful'. If we don't see ourselves as 'winning' in this 'competition' we can then experience what some have termed 'FOMO' (fear of missing out).

This can apply to our spiritual lives too - other people seem to be more spiritually successful, holier, closer to God! Our search for God often seems to end with us missing out or falling short, and our prayer life can become dry or in some cases disappear altogether. In spiritual terms we can't ever seem to get it right, to get where we want to be.

But when Jesus said he came to call sinners not the virtuous he was saying that his call is not to the perfect but the struggling. Some people say they can't be a Christian because they aren't good enough. However, the fact that we have failed so miserably is in fact the *essential* prerequisite to forging a closer connection with God. This certainly seems to be the case with most of the saints: inevitable failure and loss followed by a humble sense of their own smallness and unworthiness, ending in spiritual renewal and a newfound sense of peace and acceptance.

Once we feel we have 'made it' spiritually (like the Pharisees perhaps), then that is the time to be most concerned. If you are struggling, then be assured that you are in the perfect place to find God, and for God to find you. You don't have to be perfect, in fact it's better if you aren't.

....

Can I see my failures as an essential precondition for spiritual growth?

41

—

The Ego

*'Two men went up to the Temple to pray,
one a Pharisee, the other a tax collector. The
Pharisee stood there and said this prayer
to himself, 'I thank you, God, that I am not
grasping, unjust, adulterous like the rest of
mankind, and particularly that I am not like
this tax collector here. I fast twice a week; I
pay tithes on all I get.'*
(LUKE 18:10-12)

A study in the European Journal of Social Psychology, by Professor Roos Vonk, investigated the mindset of those who practice meditation and other forms of spiritual training. The purpose of most meditation and contemplation is to shrink the ego and promote humility - to make us less judgmental, and more accepting. However, the study found that the reverse occurred in the 3,700 participants - they exhibited signs of 'spiritual superiority' and an inflated sense of self-worth and narcissism, the exact opposite of any form of enlightenment! The study shows that although people set out with good intentions, the ego is a very powerful force within us. We have a deep-seated need to be better than others - more likeable, moral, or just more special or holier. And of course, we always want to be right! If we find ourselves doing rather well, spiritually or otherwise, the ego is watching and ready to let us know, 'you are making such great progress, so much better than everyone else!' This can lead us into a dangerous place; as Metropolitan Anthony Bloom pointed out, 'God can save the sinner, but not the saint you pretend to be'.

The ego is not to be confused with the sense of self-worth that comes from knowing that we are loved by God. The ego is that part of us that tells us we are better than others. It is obsessed with power, riches, security, position in society and how others see us. It always puts itself first, it is affronted when it feels humiliated, it becomes anxious when confronted by possible failure or loss of face and it is always fearful of losing what it thinks it has gained. It tells us that owning stuff will make us happy, and it attempts to boost our self-esteem by constantly putting others down. And the more we feed the ego, the bigger it becomes and the more it needs to be fed; and the more destructive it becomes to others and sadly, to ourselves. It resists change, it blocks humility, it is smug and arrogant, and it loves to compare itself favourably to everyone else. If our ego rules our lives, then we become vain and self-obsessed. We become control freaks. Threatened by the success of others, we hate it when people disagree with us, we feed off and yearn for praise, awards and 'pats on the back'. And if we are religious our emphasis is on individual salvation, 'heaven for me', rather than salvation for all.

But this ego-self is not our real self, what Thomas Merton calls our 'true self'. It is a 'false self', a kind of mask which hides who we really are, and who God calls us to be. Pope John Paul II put it this way, 'It is Jesus that you seek when you dream of happiness... it is He who urges you to shed the masks of false life'. Developing our spirituality is perhaps less about adding something to our self and more about taking away those parts of our false ego-driven self which hold us back and prevent us from flourishing. Most of Jesus' teachings involve some form of letting go, in order to find something better.

If we accept the fact that our worth comes from knowing that we are loved by God, then the ego can melt away. You have everything already, so you have nothing to prove to anyone. You don't need to push anyone else down in order to walk tall - you don't need to seek out anyone else's approval if you are held in the steady eternal gaze of a loving Father. You've made it! You've already hit the jackpot. This is what Jesus meant when he said, 'I have come to set you free'. God says, see yourself as I see you, and you will have a peace the world (and your ego) can never give you.

Of course, prayer and contemplation are important in the Christian life, but they must be linked with action. There can be no 'enlightenment' without action. We meet Jesus in contemplative prayer, but we also need to meet him in our daily interactions with our brothers and sisters. Small acts of selflessness and self-sacrifice destroy the ego and allow us to die to self. This is what St Paul meant when he said, 'I live now not with my own life but with the life of Christ who lives in me.' (Galatians 2:20).

....

Can I stand aside for a moment and recognise my ego, my false-self? Can I see how I might work to diminish it, and encourage the growth of my true self?

DOING CHRISTIANITY

42

—

Love yourself

'You must love your neighbour as yourself.'
(Mark 12:31)

We all know that love makes the world go round. It is what everyone seems to want, and to be searching for. Jesus gives it the utmost importance in the Gospel - it is front and centre of his teaching - the Golden Rule. Notice that Jesus says you must love your neighbour *as yourself*.

How you treat another is generally how you treat yourself. It is difficult to love others completely if you don't love and accept yourself, and if you don't love and accept yourself it is hard for you to love and accept God.

When we are comfortable in our own skin we can reach out more fully to others and to God. However, this isn't easy. As Thomas a Kempis said, 'Wherever you go, there you are'. For some, past experiences have left deep wounds and feelings of guilt or shame. This can lead someone to feel that they don't deserve the love of others, or themselves. For many, there is an inability to accept themselves as they are, struggling with their appearance perhaps, or their personality, or 'the cards that life has dealt them', constantly wishing to change themselves or be someone else. We worry about whether we are: too fat, too short, too plain, not clever enough, not funny enough, not fit enough, too old, too anxious, too shy, too exuberant, or just plain useless at everything. We fret about our clothes, are we too dowdy perhaps, not keeping up with the latest trends, or we worry that our car or lifestyle doesn't really reflect our aspirations. It's difficult to love yourself if you can't accept who you are. Moreover, many struggle because they feel they have never been loved themselves - it can be difficult to experience self-worth if you believe you have never been valued yourself.

Sometimes we set our sights too low, happy to keep our eyes on the ground, we 'think small' rather than reach for the stars - we see our limitations rather than our unlimited potential, listening too much to our 'inner critic'. Yet Jesus tells us, 'rejoice rather that your names are written in heaven' (Luke 10:20), and Psalm 139 tells us that in God's eyes we are 'wonderfully made'.

Jesus came to tell us that we are loved. As John says '... this is love. Not that we loved God but that he loved us' (1 John 4:10). Listen to the inner voice of God within. It is always loving, encouraging, optimistic and generous. If your inner voice is self-critical, condemnatory and judgemental, or conversely, arrogant, proud and boastful then be assured, such thoughts don't come from God. Sometimes we may think that we are separated from God, but remember that this is just a thought, an idea. It is not real. As St Paul said, nothing can ever separate us from the love of God.

We need to see ourselves as God sees us, love ourselves as he loves us. In order to move on from previous hurts and guilt we must leave the past behind - there must be no dwelling on things that have passed. Although we cannot forget things that have happened we can look back on the past with kindness; by accepting the love and forgiveness of God, we are enabled to leave regret and guilt behind, and start anew. As CS Lewis said, 'You can't go back and change the beginning, but you can start where you are and change the ending'.

God is always eager to wipe the slate clean and start again. If you are worthy of God's love, then you are worthy of your own self-love. If God believes in us, then we can believe in ourselves. If we find all this difficult to accept then we need to give ourselves a break, stop being so hard on ourselves. God can only love the person you are right now because that is the only you that exists at the moment. If we can say 'I'm OK, I am created and loved by God, and I'm just fine', then we can move on to the first part of Jesus' instruction and 'love our neighbour'. Our circle of love can widen and the cycle can continue, because the more love you give, the more you will receive in return.

If you find it hard to love yourself then make a conscious effort to love others. Sometimes we have to 'prime the pump', we have to begin the flow of love, and once we get started loving others we can allow that love to wash back into acceptance and love of ourself. When you have seen and loved Christ in another, you can better see and love the Christ filled person you are, your true self, worthy of unconditional love and joy.

....

Can I begin the 'flow of love' within me?

43

—

Ware tada shiru taru

'Search, and you will find...'
(MATTHEW 7:7)

At the entrance to the famous Zen Buddhist Ryoan-ji Temple in Kyoto there is a 17th century stone water basin which visitors can use to purify themselves before visiting the holy places. The four Chinese characters inscribed on the basin, 'ware tada shiru taru', can be translated as, 'I already have all I need'. For centuries this has reminded visitors of an important spiritual truth.

In modern culture we can often get sucked into believing that our happiness can only be derived from other things or other people: 'I'll be happy when I finish school, when I get a good job, when I get that house, when I meet 'The One', when I have children, when I get that promotion, when my children leave home, when I have enough cash in the bank, when my children settle down, when I stop working, when I draw my pension, when I have my operation, when I install my stair-lift ...' and so on, and so on. We can spend our lives never really getting 'all we need', so never really finding true happiness. We get the odd fleeting surge of joy, but never that feeling of underlying contentment that we are really searching for.

In times gone by Christian preachers often told people that life was a 'vale of tears', but eventually they would get their reward in heaven. We often seem to be waiting for something better to turn up, some event or relationship or possession that will make us complete, but are often disappointed. The idea that material possessions necessarily make us happy has been disproved. Bhutan has been ranked as one of the happiest countries in the world despite being one of the poorest. We must learn to love what we possess rather than possess what we love.

Unhappiness is often caused by what we think and believe. Very often we are unhappy because we tend to focus on what we lack. 'If only my current situation (or the world around me) could change, then I'd be fine'. Many of us have been taught to think in ways which limit our potential. What often needs to change is not other people or our situation, but how we think about things. And we are the only people who can control what goes on in our minds - the thoughts, beliefs and negative emotions that we allow into our headspace. If we could only let go of our attachments to these thoughts, and accept ourselves as we are, then we might be able to understand what Jesus meant when he said that the kingdom of God is close at hand, not far away. God isn't someone outside of ourselves that we can one day 'find', like a perfect-fitting pair of shoes. He's a part of us, he's already there, and always has been.

Grasping outside of ourselves for contentment rarely works because we are looking in the wrong place. Many Western searchers often travel thousands of miles to the East to seek out a 'guru' to tell them the secret of happiness when it is right under their noses.

God does not want us to go anywhere – he wants us to realise that we are *already* there (and always have been).

Accepting that we are truly blessed and already possessing all we need to live a good life enables us to reduce our attachment to things outside of ourselves and increase our reliance on God. And accepting who we truly are enables us to generously acknowledge and love those around us.

For most of us, the first step towards spiritual contentment is to accept, and then live the phrase - 'I already have all I need'.

Do I believe that 'I have all I need'?

44

—

Job Description

*'You are the light of the world ... No one lights
a lamp to put it under a tub; they put it on the
lamp-stand where it shines for everyone in the
house. In the same way your light must shine in
the sight of men, so that, seeing your good works,
they may give the praise to your Father in heaven.'*
(MATTHEW 5:14-16)

Job descriptions are interesting things. We get one when
we are initially hired, we look at it and think to ourselves,
'there is no way I can do all that!' Then you forget all
about it, and if you are lucky so does your boss, and it stays in
a filing cabinet gathering dust, never seeing the light of day
again. When Jesus walked the earth he gave his disciples, and
us, a job to do. It is exactly the same task that Jesus came to
do, and if there was a job description it would be short and
sweet - 'to bring light to the whole world'. Even though we
may consider ourselves to be of little importance, or terrible
sinners or completely useless, we have been tasked by Jesus
with this role. It comes with the job if we decide to accept the
post as 'follower of Christ'.

Jesus is the Light of the World, but here he gives us the
same title: '*You* are the light of the world'. This is what we

have signed up for. There is no boss and employee here, we are all in this together. The light of Jesus is in us.

I'm more than happy to opt for 'an easy life', going to church on a Sunday, keeping my head down and hiding any light I have under the tub. But to paraphrase Woody Allen, 'Going to church on Sunday does not make you a Christian any more than going into a garage makes you a car!'

Jesus says we must allow our good works to shine out, so that through our good actions others may catch a glimpse of the Christ light. Our role is to be a light to those around us - a light that illuminates, dispels darkness, and helps others to see The Way, The Truth and The Life. And Jesus is clear - we let this light shine not by our fancy words, ideas or good intentions, but by our 'good works'.

How can I allow my Christ Light to shine for others to see?

45

—

Don't worry

'you worry and fret about so many things,
and yet few are needed...'
(Luke 10:41)

A recent UK survey by the Mental Health Foundation found that at some point in the previous twelve months, almost three-quarters of adults felt so stressed that they felt overwhelmed or unable to cope. Half of the young people surveyed reported that 'comparing themselves to others' was a source of great stress. A US survey found that 48% of people have trouble sleeping because of anxiety.

We think of stress as a modern phenomenon, but worry was undoubtedly a major issue in Jesus' time and he comes back to this issue again and again. The worries of the disciples may have been different to those we experience today, but stress is nothing new in the human condition.

Jesus says that few worries are needed. He asks us to consider 'the birds in the sky. They do not sow or reap or gather into barns; yet your heavenly Father feeds them. Are you not worth much more than they are?' His message is one of calm acceptance, of relaxation - trust in God for you are precious in his eyes, he knows what you need and he will look after you. Worry is futile and pointless: 'Can any of you, says Jesus, 'for all his worrying, add one single cubit to his span of life?' Jesus tells us to 'set your hearts on his Kingdom first', focus on being the best person you can possibly be, and leave everything else in God's hands. Sometimes we have to realise that we can't always make everything right, fix things or rescue others (or ourselves). But God can.

If we worry it is often because we are trying to control everything. Jesus says in effect, 'you can't do it on your own, give up control - trust me'.

My mum used to say that when things are dreadful and you feel overwhelmed (and also when everything is wonderful) remember that *this too shall pass*. All our anxieties pass away in the fullness of time. And as for the future, well Jesus put it thus, 'do not worry about tomorrow: tomorrow will take care of itself.'

....

Can I place my trust in God? Can I believe that 'every hair on my head has been counted', that God knows me inside out, and will always take care of me? Take a moment now to reach out and place any worries you may have into the hands of a God who loves you.

46

Take up your cross

*'If anyone wants to be a follower of mine,
let him renounce himself and take up his
cross and follow me.'*
(MATTHEW 16:24-25)

Nobody ever said that life would be easy. At some point all of us will experience loss, sadness and pain, and for some these experiences can last a lifetime. The pain of grief for example can be overwhelming; the price we pay for having experienced love is the sorrow that comes when it is taken away.

There have been various explanations of Jesus' words above. One interpretation is that Jesus is acknowledging that there are burdens in life we must shoulder, but these should not prevent us from discipleship. Broken relationships, illness or having to care for a sick family member for example, should not stop us from becoming a follower of Christ. By accepting our situation and trusting in God, the burden of carrying such crosses can be eased. Jesus says: 'my yoke is easy and my burden is light'. The invitation here is to let Jesus shoulder your burden too, the one who carried his own cross to Calvary is offering to help you carry yours. In the words of Pope Francis, 'There is no cross, big or small, in our life which the Lord does not share with us'.

Another interpretation is that by taking up the cross we are surrendering ourselves to the will of God, accepting our role as his disciple. We are dying to self, and finding out who we really are and why we are here. Taking up our cross can be a positive action - loving the unloved, reaching out to that person that everyone else ignores, volunteering in a soup kitchen. Perhaps we have never thought of things this way - 'denying ourself' to help another, and in the process, finding self-fulfilment. Taking up the cross is not about losing our life; it is about finding it - and finding it in new and surprising ways and places we never thought existed.

Rather than allowing Jesus to help us carry our cross, we are in this way, helping Jesus to carry his.

....

Is there a cross I can carry for Christ?

47

Anger

*Jesus then went into the Temple and drove out
all those who were selling and buying there;
he upset the tables of the money changers and
the chairs of those who were selling pigeons.
'According to scripture' he said 'my house
will be called a house of prayer; but you are
turning into a robber's den.'*
(MATTHEW 21:12-14)

When was the last time you got angry? Can you remember what it was about? Was it a useful emotion - did it help in the situation you found yourself in?

Psychologists often tend to regard anger as a negative emotion. It often means we are out of control, hence the phrase 'losing it'. When the red mist descends we tend to live in the 'Land of Stupid' - we think stupid things, say stupid things and do stupid things. Very often we look back on our anger the next day and think, 'why did I say that', or 'why did I do that?' And of course, there is always the danger that anger can turn to violence, spite and hatred.

There is one famous recorded incident of Jesus getting angry in the Gospels. The money changers and merchants had taken over the temple, 'his Father's house', and turned it into a market-place. Jesus upsets their tables and chairs and drives them out. It is certainly not an image one would normally associate with the traditional notion of the 'gentle Jesus'. We also see flashes of anger when Jesus confronts the scribes and Pharisees: 'you hypocrites', 'alas for you blind guides' he says. When the Pharisees refused to answer Jesus' questions about whether it was right to cure a man with a withered hand on the Sabbath, Mark records that, 'grieved to find them so obstinate, he looked angrily at them.'

Jesus' anger does not appear to be out of control. His anger was directed at sinfulness, hypocrisy and injustice rather than at any individual person. It was not about him or any perceived slight against him. Even though he was angry at the hypocrisy of the Pharisees he still loved them (their behaviour 'grieved him') and he wanted them to change. Jesus shows us that anger in itself is not always self-centred and destructive - there is such a thing as righteous anger.

There are many things that should make us angry: people going hungry in a world when there is enough food for everyone if it was only shared out fairly; the exploitation of people in order to line the pockets of the rich and powerful; the 'do-nothing' approach of world leaders and business to the impending catastrophe of climate change; the incarceration of millions of people around the globe on account of their ethnicity or religion; racism and all forms of prejudice and discrimination; domestic violence and child exploitation. There is a long list, and if these things don't make us angry then we need to look closely at ourselves, and what our priorities are. Righteous anger can and should lead us to action. If there is no righteous anger then there is often just passivity - we become 'bystanders' whilst others suffer.

Perhaps Jesus driving the money changers from the Temple is just the example we need to get us off our sofas and take action?

....

What makes me angry and (more importantly) what can I do about it?

48

—

Pride

'He has shown the power of his arm, he has routed the proud of heart. He has pulled down princes from their thrones and exalted the lowly.'
(LUKE 1:51-52)

There has been controversy in recent years over the Last Night of the Proms in London. Some commentators feel that there is too much jingoism in anthems such as 'Rule, Britannia!', whilst others argue that we should be 'proud to be British'. Certainly in UK schools now, teachers are encouraged to show children that it is good to have pride in Britain, and to celebrate the 'British values' of tolerance, democracy, liberty and respect for others. So is pride a virtue or a sin?

The problem arises when this pride morphs into a view that your country is superior to all other nations, 'My country right or wrong'. 'Pride in the nation' has probably led to more wars and conflict in history than anything else. Similarly, a pride in one's religion which demeans the faith of others has resulted in violence, mistrust and persecution.

Leaving this aside, pride is concerned primarily with the individual. It is said to be the first of the so-called 'Seven

Deadly Sins', the gateway through which all other sins arrive. St. Augustine said that, 'It was pride that changed angels into devils', and St Thomas Aquinas wrote that, 'inordinate self-love is the cause of every sin'. However, pride is not to be confused with self-respect or appropriate self-esteem as a child of God. Nor is pride to be equated with proper self-love - we are called to love our neighbour *as ourselves*.

Pride consists of thinking that we are better than others; it is self-centred and looks down on neighbour. If we are looking down on another, then we cannot lift our eyes to see the Christ within. Pride inflates a person's self-importance and diminishes the importance of those around them. Moreover, pride and vanity are two sides of the same coin - a vain person is obsessed with their appearance; they are concerned not so much with their inward character but with their ability to turn heads (or receive awards and public praise). This can often lead them to disparage others in order to elevate themselves to a higher place of honour. If we have beauty or intelligence, they are gifts from God. St Paul pointed out to the arrogant Corinthians, 'What do you have that was not given to you? And if it was given, how can you boast as though it were not?' (Cor 4:7-8).

Pride destroys both self and others. Proverbs tells us that 'pride goes before a fall'. Moreover, a proud person is too obsessed with self to genuinely care for, or empathize with, another. There is no need of others, or God, if you believe that you are totally self-sufficient and the master of your own destiny. It also leads to envy - if we are filled with self-pride then it is inevitable that we will covet and desire the things another has that we feel we lack.

True humility is the antidote to pride. This does not mean that we think less of ourselves - it is about thinking of ourselves less. It is about replacing self-centeredness with self-lessness.

It is about recognising our faults and weaknesses without letting them eat away at our self-worth. Humility means recognising that we are sinful, whilst still remembering that we are loved and cherished by God and forgiven by him.

....

We all need to make it easier for other people to love us – make a start today by releasing your pride and admitting your mistakes.

49

—

Past and present

'Consider the lilies of the field...'
(MATTHEW 6:28-29)

Wisdom can be found in many places (not just the Bible), and children's animated films contain some classic lines, including this gem from *Kung Fu Panda 2*: 'Yesterday is history, tomorrow is a mystery, but today is a gift. That's why it's called the present!'

Why do we find it so hard to live in the present? If we are not careful we can end up wishing we were a different person, in a different place, doing something different, with someone else!

We are conditioned by our past, and we often return to it in negative ways, pondering over past failures, often wading through oceans of regret. We are also obsessed with the future, creating scenarios where one day all our troubles will be over. Often the present moment is either just a replay of past events, or a looking forward to what might happen in the days to come, some future salvation perhaps, or an escape from an unfulfilling present? How many of us are just wishing our lives away?

The present moment is all there is - the rest is an illusion. This is what is meant by the phrase 'wake up and smell the roses'; becoming aware of, and appreciating, the beauty of the world around us. *This moment* is the only thing that matters. Whatever you have done in the past has gone, whatever worship, prayer, good or not so good deeds you have done, all have gone, and cannot be altered. As Isaiah says, there is 'No need to recall the past, no need to think about what was done before.' And whatever things you will do tomorrow are, as yet, undone. The only time you can connect with God and the world is now.

When we are fully present we often find that judgement and anxiety disappear. What is the point of continually blaming ourselves for past mistakes, or getting anxious about what is to come? When Jesus said, 'consider the lilies of the field', he was saying, 'you don't need to worry, everything is under my control, all is well'. In a sense, you could argue that not living in the present is not living at all. It's certainly not living 'life to the full'. It's hard to reach out to God when our minds are not in the moment, when we are fretting over past mistakes or future problems. We often create worries 'out of nothing' and sometimes we *choose* to have a problem and all the anxiety that follows, rather than accepting the promise of Jesus - 'come to me all you who labour and I will give you rest'. And of course, if we don't release pain we often just end up passing it on to other people.

Jean-Pierre de Caussade, author of 'The Sacrament of the Present Moment' puts it like this: 'The present moment holds infinite riches beyond your wildest dreams ... The will of God presents itself at each moment like an immense ocean.'

Am I willing to step into the ocean of the present moment?

50

—

Change yourself

*Do not model yourselves on the behaviour of
the world around you, but let your behaviour
change, modelled by your new mind.*
(ROMANS 12:2)

When I was a teacher in a sixth form college I was sometimes asked to talk to young men (and occasionally women) who had become very angry. The reason was almost always because another student had 'disrespected them'. Their sense of self, generally macho and alpha male, had been damaged by the words of another. It often took quite a while to 'talk them down', to let them see that the 'big man' walks away, that it is fragility not strength that allows another to disturb your inner peace and sense of who you are.

Human beings hurt each other. It doesn't matter what religion we belong to - Christians hurt each other just as much as Muslims and Hindus. Those with no faith are often no worse or better than those who believe. We also hurt ourselves by our own self-destructive behaviour and impulses. Each day Christ sufferers and is crucified again by what we do to one another (and to ourselves).

Often this hurt is a direct result of religion. Throughout history people have hurt one another in the name of God. We use our holy books to condemn each other, to judge and often to oppress. The Bible has often been used as a weapon of control rather than a manual of love. At times we actively seek out conflict and division, rather than harmony and agreement. We look for reasons to oppose and discriminate, rather than unify and include. This makes us unable to see the goodness in the other - it polarises us, entrenches division, spawns hate. If you doubt this, just take a look at recent political campaigns in the Western democracies. So often religions, nations, political parties, ethnic groups and communities behave like a sixth form student - someone has 'disrespected them' and they must respond in kind. Sometimes people even feel the need to respond to protect 'God's honour' when they feel he has been disrespected. Blasphemy laws may have fallen into disuse in the West, but they are alive and kicking in many parts of the globe. We behave as if God is so small he needs us to 'protect' him.

Whilst we 'crucify Christ' every day, his response is to offer us freedom. His Gospel frees us from a self-centred way of thinking which says that we need to protect our fragile ego by attacking someone else.

Jesus' message to his disciples is simple - instead of trying to change everybody else, we must start changing ourselves, and when this change leads us to love others, we change the world. But changing ourselves is not a pre-requisite of God's love for us. Jesus doesn't tell his disciples that he will only love them if they change. He knows that by loving them, they *can* change. We are called to do the same.

And that is all that really matters - as St John of the Cross said, 'At the evening of this life, we shall be judged on our love'.

....

Our task is to find God in our daily struggles with life and let him change us. What needs to change in me?

51

—

What does your heart choose?

'Set your hearts on his kingdom first, and on his righteousness, and all these other things will be given you as well.'
(Matthew 6:33)

Asking friends 'How are you' is something we often say after we have said 'Hello'. We expect them to say, 'fine thank you' and then move on to discuss the weather or the football. I once asked a colleague at work 'how are you' and he said, 'I am choosing to be well.' I thought it an odd thing to say. However, as a teacher of psychology and biology he understood that the choices we make in our mind very often determine the health of our bodies.

For years psychologists have argued over whether people are shaped primarily by their genetic inheritance or by their environment (nature vs nurture). Are we who we are because of our DNA, or because of our upbringing and the trends and influences affecting us each day? Those favouring nature point to studies of twins who have been separated at birth and adopted by very different families, who end up with similar personal characteristics, careers and lifestyles. Those on the side of nurture point to how our early childhood up-bringing and parental love, or lack of it, shape the adult we become; this allegedly prompted St Ignatius to say, 'Give me a child until he is seven and I will show you the man'.

Whatever we might think of this debate my teacher friend was definitely on to something. Each day we face a series of choices based on free will. Some aspects of our life may be constrained by circumstances, for example we may *have* to go to work to feed our family, but *how* we go out to work is within our choice.

As we come to the end of Step 3 and our consideration of 'Who Am I?' it is perhaps worth summarising some of the choices we are faced with every day that make us who we are.

When we take our first deep breath on waking, do we choose to see that breath as God's breath of life, sustaining us and bringing us to a new dawn? As we turn on the tap to wash, do we choose to see the gift of water provided by God to enable all life on the planet to survive? Do we recognise the food on our breakfast table as God's gift to us, and ac-knowledge with gratitude, the hard work of our brothers and sisters who have enabled us to receive it? Do we choose to see the people we meet in our day as our brothers and sis-ters in Christ, seeing the good in those we encounter? In our homes or places of work do we choose to apply St. Benedict's monastic rule: 'all guests who present themselves are to be welcomed as Christ?' Can we understand that our daily hu-miliations and disappointments are opportunities to dimin-ish our ego and develop the grace of humility? Do we choose to see suffering as our teacher, recognising the opportuni-ties to learn in every apparent setback? Can we see the hand of God in the unexpected and surprising - am I grateful for what I have been given or do I choose to be constantly crav-ing more? Do we choose to see the handiwork of God not just in the awesome beauty of lakes and mountains but in our city streets and squares - seeing the grandeur of God in a weed poking up from the pavement?

Have I chosen to see myself at the mercy of life's forces, tossed around like a small boat on a vast uncertain ocean, or am I, through the gift of free will, in charge of my own destiny and my own choices, under the gaze of a God who loves me? Am I choosing to live in the present moment letting go of past hurts and pain, or do I continue to carry around burdens and guilt from a past which is gone forever and cannot be changed? Do I choose to be anxious about my future rather than trusting in God that 'all will be well'? Am I able to believe that I am of value and worthy of God's love, and do I extend this belief to all I meet; do I put into practice the gospel of Jesus or just pay lip service to it on a Sunday?

There is much that is outside our control, but we can decide the way we *react* to life's events.

....

What choices am I making in the way I react to the daily events of my life?

STEP FOUR

A New Way of Seeing

The Jesuit theologian, Fr Anthony de Mello, said that spirituality means waking up: 'Most people, even though they don't know it, are asleep. They're born asleep, they live asleep, they marry in their sleep, they breed children in their sleep, they die in their sleep, without ever waking up. They never understand the loveliness and the beauty of this thing that we call human existence.' (*On Spirituality and Waking Up*).

Our Fourth Step is about waking up to a new way of looking at the world - opening our eyes to a new vision and a new set of possibilities. For many Christians the Bible has been reduced to a set of doctrines rather than an invitation to a new way of seeing. In the Gospel extracts which follow we learn that an encounter with Christ is always an invitation to see things differently. For some of us this can involve 'unlearning' lots of things we may have previously understood or been taught. As Jesus said, we need 'eyes to see' (and ears to hear).

52

—

Looking and Seeing

'Have you eyes that do not see, ears that do not hear?'
(MARK 8:18-19)

I once needed to find my reading glasses to study some very small print, and I was annoyed when I couldn't find them. I searched in all the usual places where I might have put them, but it was fruitless. It was then that I touched my face and discovered that the glasses were in fact on my nose. Not on the top of my head, they were on my nose - I was wearing them. I found them in the place where they always were. The story tells you three things about me: I can't read very small print with my reading glasses, I am often absent minded, and I sometimes can't see what's on the end of my nose - I can't see for looking.

It's not supposed to be difficult to find God. He isn't playing hide and seek with us, and it's not a game which only the chosen few can play; it's an equal opportunities endeavour. Sadly, we often enclose God in our churches, rituals and worship, and we never get to see him anywhere else. Yet he is everywhere in creation; he can't make himself more visible. From our first breath of the morning till our eyes close and sleep descends, and then throughout the night - he is there. Creation is soaked and suffused with the splendour of God. I'm not just talking here about the mountains, lakes and seashore, but every aspect of every day. The flower in the garden, the rain beating on the rooftop, the light shining through the window pane, the child playing in the park, the spider constructing his web of extraordinary complexity and beauty - a feat of exquisite engineering.

A walk in the forest, or just looking at a solitary tree can provoke as much loving wonder and awe as gazing up at the architectural masterpieces of our most ancient churches.

In his encyclical letter, 'Laudato Si', Pope Francis says: 'the divine and the human meet in the slightest detail in the seamless garment of God's creation, in the last speck of dust of our planet'. God is in every speck of dust! Pierre Teilhard de Chardin put it this way: 'Christ, through his Incarnation, is interior to the world, rooted in the world even in the very heart of the tiniest atom.' God isn't some-where else, he's all around us.

Consider your body for a moment, the eyes flicking across the page, taking in all this information which your brain pro-cesses effortlessly. Look at your hands, the movement in the fingers, the lines on your palm and the nails growing imper-ceptibly. The wonder of creation is God's masterpiece, and he is ever present. The God of love has made his home in the universe, and he is there within you, and in all we meet. Theologians like to discuss the 'problem of evil', but it might be better to understand the 'problem of goodness' – how come there is so much universal and persistent goodness in the world? Our focus is often on 'original sin' rather than 'original goodness' – 'God saw all that he had made, and it was very good' (Genesis 1:31).

Many of us mistakenly believe that we only receive the

sacraments from a priest in a church. But the world around us is nothing less than another sacrament, a visible expression of the reality of God and a channel for his grace. In 'Laudato Si', Pope Francis says, 'As Christians we are called to accept the world as a sacrament of communion'. God takes every opportunity to connect with us, wherever we are and whatever we are doing, and such grace is freely given.

According to St. Bonaventure, 'God's fingerprints' are everywhere. Human love, forgiveness and compassion is divine love, forgiveness and compassion. Our concerns and joys are God's concerns and joys; our journey is God's journey. This is the incarnation today, Christ enfleshed in the ordinary moments of our day, God connecting with us in all our human experiences. And of course we can only ever experience God in the here-and-now.

Being a Christian isn't primarily about going to church or believing in doctrine. *A Christian is a person who sees Christ in other people.* Jesus is constantly telling his followers to stop sleep-walking, to wake up and see a new vision of the world – the kingdom of God. Try looking at the world today with a fresh pair of eyes, look at things as if for the first time. God is unchanging, we are the ones who need to change - can we see the holy, the goodness of God that is already there, right in front of our noses?

If we choose not to see him (and we often only see what we want to see), then that ultimately is our decision, and Jesus knew this when he said, let those who have eyes to see, see.

It's not so hard to find God if you know where to look - and where to look is *everywhere*.

We can connect with God at any time by just being fully present to what is right in front of us. Spend a few moments today appreciating the goodness or beauty of something close to you - something very simple such as the palm of your hand, a tree, a child's laughter, a cup of tea or the sun shining through the clouds. Just pause and contemplate this for a while. Then expand this realisation to encompass the whole of God's creation - see the goodness and beauty of everything and everyone, including you. Move from the small, specific thing to the universal and all-embracing reality. Spend some time with this thought. God is good, and he has created a world of awesome beauty and wonder, and you are lucky enough to have been chosen to be a part of it (and it a part of you). We are, each of us, a vital and unique part of the universe, tasked with co-creating a world of goodness and beauty. The kingdom of heaven is at hand, the kingdom of heaven is in our hands.

53

—

Fear and Joy

May the God of hope bring you such joy and
peace in your faith that the power of the Holy
Spirit will remove all bounds to hope.
(ROMANS 15:13)

At my Catholic primary school the class would be taken to church on a regular basis so that we could confess our sins to a priest. Any Catholic over a certain age will probably know what I mean. At that tender age most of us couldn't think of many sins, so we often had to make them up. Two or three were expected for each confession (I am reliably informed that around half of all confessed sins involve 'missing Mass on Sunday'). I always went to Mass, but two regulars on my 'sin laundry list' were 'being disobedient' and 'telling lies'. It is ironic that my confession of 'telling lies' was (most of the time) a lie! In fact telling the priest 'I told lies' was occasionally my only lie of the week! Fortunately the priest would never quiz us about anything we said (not with a class of 35 to get through). After we received absolution we would be told to do a penance - 'say 3 Hail Marys'. Sadly, this reinforced the notion that God's forgiveness wasn't freely given but dependent on some kind of payback from me, like paying a fine in court. One day a visiting priest told me my penance was to 'do something to help your Mum when you get home'. Good idea, but as a nine year old I definitely preferred the 3 Hail Mary option! All this was a rather fearful experience, none of us found it healing or uplifting, and certainly not particularly sacramental. Thankfully it's no longer a weekly event for pupils in our Catholic schools.

It does however explain why many people have been 'turned off' religion. The church of the past was largely founded on fear. It was obsessed with sin, and certain sins would be punished with eternal damnation. It fostered guilt, and often appeared more focused on power and control than preaching a gospel of love. The theology behind this worldview was dark, bleak, judgmental and petty - anyone outside the church could not be saved, and there was nothing we could learn from our brothers and sisters in other Christian denominations, and certainly not from those of other faiths.

In essence there are two ways of looking at Christianity. The first involves demands and obligations: 'Believe this, do that, and you will be saved.' The second involves relationship and 'metanoia' (a transformative change of heart). The first is a warning, the second an invitation.

This first view is increasingly disappearing. We are reclaiming the theology of the early church. The world is a good place. God shares in our sorrows and joys; he is our constant guide and encourager. He picks us up when we fall, his love is unconditional and endless. This isn't a new theology; it is there on every page of the gospel - Jesus came to heal us not punish us. Thomas Aquinas said, 'God is sheer joy'. Today we are rediscovering the joy, light and hope of the gospel, something that disappeared from our churches for far too long.

....

What needs to be refreshed in my own theological outlook?

54

—

Open your eyes

Then Jesus spoke, 'What do you want me
to do for you?' 'Master' the blind man said
to him 'Master, let me see again'. Jesus
said to him, 'Go; your faith has saved you'.
And immediately his sight returned and he
followed him along the road.
(MARK 10:51)

Jesus' first words to Bartimaeus, the blind man are: 'What
do you want me to do for you?' If Jesus posed that question today, how would you reply? Our first response
might be to ask for a pay rise or a lottery win! On reflection
we might say, 'I want to be happy', and then wonder how this
is to be achieved. Bartimaeus simply wants to 'see again'. In
spite of, or because of, his personal darkness, he believes and
hopes in Jesus. His disability has not caused him to lose faith;
he clearly knows who Jesus is, and when he hears him passing
by he shouts loudly 'Jesus have pity on me'. In this cry we hear
the echo of many of those who are suffering in the world.

We often grope our way through life, eyes half closed. We
can sometimes be blind to the pain of those around us, we
often fail to see what is in our own best interests, or what it is
that will give us lasting joy. We can stumble blindly through

life, never really waking up to what we are doing, or where we are going.

Life is not just what we can see. Jesus heals the blind man. But then the Gospel tells us that Bartimaeus got up and followed Jesus along the road. Jesus doesn't just return his sight - he then gives him a purpose, by letting him see the Christ Light. He gives him hope in a hurting world. Note that Jesus doesn't ask him to sign up to a creed or set of doctrinal propositions, he isn't getting him to join a club. He simply wants Bartimaeus to follow him along the narrow path.

Bartimaeus knows what his mission is now, to become a disciple of Christ, and by doing so he turns the original question on its head, and asks Jesus: 'What do you want me to do for you?'

....

What is my response to Jesus' question: 'What do you want me to do for you?'

55

—

Live life to the full

*'I have come so that they may have life and
have it to the full.'*
(JOHN 10:10)

When I was in my early twenties I worked for a while in the guesthouse of a Dominican convent in the south of France as a washer-up and cleaner. One day whilst I was sweeping the floor in the lobby, Sister Brigitte approached me and said she thought I was doing it all wrong. Being fairly proud of my skill with a dustpan and brush I asked how she thought I could improve my technique. She asked me: "are you enjoying yourself?" "Not really," I replied. "That's where you're going wrong", she said. When I was doing the washing-up later, it occurred to me that I wasn't enjoying that either. How could I enjoy all the activities of daily life no matter how mundane? That was the challenge Brigitte had set me – to see the mundane activities of my work in a different way. Today we might call this mindfulness - fully living in, and appreciating, the present moment, and being grateful for the gift of being alive.

Another French nun St. Therese of Lisieux developed her spirituality of the 'Little Way' before she died at the age of twenty-four. Therese said that we don't need to perform 'great deeds' in order to find God. The everyday events of life can be made holy if they are done with a loving heart for the greater glory of God. Cooking dinner, washing dishes, going to work – such activities can be a path to holiness, indeed any job or task however menial can be holy if we insist that it is so. According to Therese, God's love is made manifest in our world when we do the little things in a loving way. God is everywhere, present in the smallest details of our ordinary lives. The smallest action however insignificant, done with love, is more important than 'great things' done for personal glory or fame. 'Everything is grace' she said, meaning that God is present in each of us and every thing, enabling us to do the ordinary things in life with extraordinary love. This is how Almighty God comes to us - disguised as the ordinary!

Jesus didn't necessarily come to teach us how to be super-holy or saintly; he came to show us how to be an authentic human being, how to be comfortable in our created skin, how to live fully as a child of God, formed in his image and likeness. This is what Jesus meant by 'living life to the full', and it is something that is within the reach of all of us.

If you want to know where God is you don't necessarily need to look to the highest heaven, visit a cathedral, buy a Bible or read a catechism. Look for him in the ordinary events of your daily life. He is to be found in all the unpredictable, mundane everyday experiences we encounter. Find him here and you will find him everywhere - he isn't hiding from us.

....

Be fully present when you wash-up today or clean your teeth! Become aware of the presence of God in your everyday activities, however mundane or boring they may appear to be on the surface.

If you wish to know more about St Therese's spirituality take a look at 'The Little Way Association', who work to help the needy in the developing world – putting into practice Therese's promise to 'spend her heaven doing good on earth'. (www.littlewayassociation.com).

56

—

Picking corn

*'The sabbath was made for man, not man for
the sabbath.'*
(MARK 2:27-28)

Pope Francis got into big trouble in 2018 when he married a couple on board a plane in a flight over Chile. Some conservative commentators asked whether the relevant paperwork had been submitted, had the couple attended a marriage preparation course, and was the bishop in the diocese they were flying over informed? The Pope said later that those complaining should be told that the couple, 'were prepared and I made a judgement call. The sacraments are for people.'

Mark tells us that the Pharisees were annoyed that Jesus' disciples were picking and eating corn on the sabbath, which was forbidden. Jesus tells them that the sabbath was made for man, not the other way round, and concludes that 'the Son of Man is master even of the sabbath'. The disciples were hungry, and Jesus put that common-sense reality before the ritual demands of the Pharisees. Sometimes we can allow rules and regulations to come before humanity. Religious leaders often use rules to maintain their power and control over others. We can do that too, seeking comfort in certainty, and maintaining our own sense of control by trying to control others. Like the Pharisees we can be adept at pointing out the flaws in those around us.

Authoritarianism appears in all religions, and whenever it attempts to crush mercy and common-sense we must remember that Jesus always sees the bigger picture and puts the needs of his people before the legalism and finger wagging of the Pharisees. This echoes the verse in Matthew's Gospel: 'a bruised reed he will not break'. Unlike the power often exercised by man, the power of Jesus flows from gentleness and compassion.

Anthony de Mello describes a story told by the late Archbishop of Milan, Cardinal Martini. After their wedding (in Italy) a couple asked their parish priest if they could have their reception in the church instead of the parish courtyard, because it was starting to pour with rain. The priest was reluctant but was eventually persuaded to allow it. Wine was drunk, cake was eaten, songs were sung and more wine was drunk. The priest, upset at the noise they were making in the House of God, complains to his assistant, who then tells him, 'we mustn't forget Father, that Jesus himself was once present at a wedding reception in Cana!' Father replies indignantly, 'I know Jesus was present at Cana! But they didn't have the Blessed Sacrament there!'

....

What do you take away from Cardinal Martini's story?

57

—

You did it to me

'I was hungry and you gave me food; I was thirsty and you gave me drink; I was a stranger and you made me welcome; naked and you clothed me, sick and you visited me, in prison and you came to see me ... I tell you solemnly in so far as you did this to one of the least of these brothers of mine, you did it to me.'
(MATTHEW 25:35-40)

If you need persuading that religion is about what you do, rather than what you think or believe, then these are verses to ponder. It is a manifesto for *action*. Jesus is letting us know that he is present in everybody, everywhere. He is in the tabernacle and the church, but he is also hidden in humanity - living, suffering, feeling pain, enduring loneliness and dying. He lives in each of us; in the words of Mother Teresa, we are all 'Jesus in disguise'. We search 'high and low' for God, and yet here he is, right under our noses. If you want to know where God is then look no further than the person sitting next to you, the lonely neighbour nobody talks to, the child in a refugee camp with no running water, the families who go hungry each day in the poorest countries of the world. When we perform acts of kindness and mercy to others, we do such actions to Christ himself. And conversely, when we fail to love, when we ignore, when we 'cross the road', when we complain of compassion fatigue, then we neglect, and at worst reject Jesus. For the Christian there is no longer any excuse to ignore 'the least of them'.

This is what the incarnation does - it places Christ in our midst, and we become Christ for others. As St Simeon wrote, 'These hands of mine are the hands of God; this body of mine is the body of God because of the incarnation'. God's home is now in us, and our relationship with Him is inseparable from our relationship with everyone and everything. God is present in every personal experience and encounter if only we had the eyes to see it. And this awareness changes everything.

As an aside, if you find Sunday worship or the sacraments dull or uninspiring then start to see God in the everyday experiences you have. If you struggle to see him in the daily events of your life, then you will find it hard to experience him on a Sunday. Conversely, when we see God all around us then our sacramental worship can come alive.

Notice that in the extract from Matthew, no-one is getting a medal for their *beliefs*, there is no 'pat on the back' for those with the 'correct theology'. Jesus is saying that it is loving kindness that has the eternal significance. As always Jesus puts actions before philosophy. And his focus is on each person doing what is right. He wants us to stop thinking about and judging the thoughts and actions of others, and focus on what we ourselves are doing - are you feeding the hungry, welcoming the stranger, visiting the sick?

We all hold our own particular prejudices, and it is sometimes hard to see Christ in certain people, perhaps those we think 'have brought their trouble on themselves', or those we regard as enemies. When we can begin to see Jesus in these people, then we are seeing with the eyes of Christ, and not our own. It is both unsettling, and a comfort, to know that Christ's presence is universal - we don't get to choose where Jesus lives. He simply is.

This is a crucial part of Jesus' message - you, me, Him - there is no distinction, we are all one, all the same.

Knowing this is one thing, living it quite another. If everybody could see God living in one another, especially in the wounded, and act accordingly, what a world we would create! There would be no war, no violence, no loneliness. Hunger would be eliminated. As Gandhi said: 'The world has enough for everyone's need, but not enough for everyone's greed'. It has been shown that we could easily feed the world, but we don't.

As always, when we start to put Jesus' teaching into practice, we not only enable personal change and salvation for ourselves, but we also help bring about social change and justice for all.

....

See if you can encounter Christ in those you meet today.

58

—

God within

*Do you acknowledge that Jesus Christ is
really in you?*
(2 Corinthians 13:5)

At school my PE teacher said he wanted to introduce
us to as many sports as possible. He said, 'You might
have the talent to be an Olympic badminton gold
medallist, but if nobody ever puts a racket in your hand you
will never know. Each of you might have some undiscov-
ered potential lying deep within you, waiting to be revealed.'
Sometimes we can't see things within us unless someone
points them out.

If we think that God is somewhere 'up above' then we
spend our lives looking upwards, or trying to get 'up there'
ourselves. It's a pre-Christian image of God, and it misses the
whole point of Christianity – God 'came down' and dwells
among us; we need to look around, not above.

In the early church St Paul emerges as the great apostle,
constantly encouraging others through his preaching and letters. Perhaps his greatest contribution to the ongoing devel-
opment of the Jesus movement was his constant reminder
to the early followers that 'Christ lives in you'. Paul wasn't
speaking in metaphor here - he meant that Christ is literally

living within each of us. God is not remote, living in the 'highest heaven' and occasionally coming to our aid when the going gets tough. He is a constant, ever-present presence within each of us - we are a 'temple of the Holy Spirit'. Paul puts it like this in Colossians 3:11, 'There is only Christ: he is everything and he is in everything.' This presence is not something we earn, or something that magically appears when we are baptized or when we say 'Jesus is Lord'. We don't earn it by good deeds, or by embracing a set of beliefs. There was never a time when Christ did not live in us, and there will never be a moment when he deserts us. Christ lives in us by virtue of our humanity.

We are all - you, me, everyone and everything - the way God is present in the world. How could it be any different: all things created by God, suffused with grace. God is everywhere. If you don't believe in God, then this doesn't suddenly make him disappear. He won't leave us if we sin, he won't snub us if we fail to acknowledge his presence. He is pure love, a love that cannot be spoilt or sullied by our actions. We can go our whole lives without ever acknowledging he is there, but his indwelling does not depend on our belief or lack of it, and he does not dwell more in Christians than others. Those who cry 'Lord, Lord' are loved no more than those who never utter a prayer. Performing marvellous good works will not make him love us more. Unlike many parents, God has no favourite child.

There is nothing we can do to make God love us more - we are his children, and always will be. In God we live and move and have our being (Acts 17:28). Don't look for God somewhere 'out there' but discover him in your deepest self, where he has always been. In the words of the Church Father, Maximus the Confessor, 'Those who seek the Lord should not look for Him outside themselves; on the contrary, they must seek Him within themselves'.

Paul goes on to say, 'In your minds you must be the same as Christ Jesus' (Philippians 2:5). God does not just want us to acknowledge his presence, he wants us to 'be like him' (1 John 3:2). We are being asked not just to admire the teaching of Jesus but to conform ourselves to the mind of Christ; to recognise his indwelling spirit *and make it our own*. In Ephesians 3:16-20 Paul describes how our 'hidden self' (not our ego-centred self) must grow strong, 'so that Christ may live in your hearts through faith'. He goes on to say that 'planted in love and built on love' we will then know 'the love of Christ which is beyond all knowledge' and be 'filled with the utter fullness of God'. That is some promise - to be filled with the utter fullness of God. The result for Paul was that 'I live now not with my own life but with the life of Christ who lives in me' (Galatians 2:20).

Humans need to experience things and to love, but it's not so easy to relate to an idea, a power or a force. However, through the incarnation of Jesus, God becomes a person, someone with a body and a face, someone with whom we can have a personal relationship.

Many of us never realise or recognise the extraordinary fact that God dwells within us. We never consciously call upon his mercy, ask for his forgiveness, or pray to be moved by the Spirit. For some the relationship is always one way. Jesus came to show us that the relationship can be two-way. He came to show us who God is. God became man so we could put a face to a name and enter into a relationship with the One who dwells within us.

God loves us, and when we open our eyes and ears to his presence, when we see him in ourselves and in others, we can begin to return that love. What was once one-way only, can begin to become two-way. We are coming home, and can finally understand Jesus' words to the disciples at The Last

Supper: 'In a short time the world will no longer see me; but you will see me, because I live and you will live. On that day you will understand that I am in my Father and you in me and I in you.' (John 14:19-20)

....

How would my life be different if I acknowledged that Christ was 'really in me'?

59

The Kingdom of God

Asked by the Pharisees when the kingdom of God was to come, he gave them this answer, 'The coming of the kingdom of God does not admit of observation and there will be no one to say, "Look here! Look there!" For, you must know, the kingdom of God is among you.'
(LUKE 17:20-21)

I t's interesting that the gospel writers record Jesus using the term 'kingdom of God' or 'kingdom of heaven' over one hundred times, and the word 'church' just twice. That might give us a sense of his priorities.

The Pharisees were always trying to catch Jesus out - their questioning appears to be designed to get him to say something which they can then use against him, but Jesus never falls into this trap. They asked him when the kingdom of God is going to come. Perhaps they were after a specific date, hoping that when it passed they could then expose Jesus as a charlatan. Or maybe they were trying to tie Jesus to a political revolution. Jesus' answer is to say that the kingdom is not going to come in the way you are expecting. The Romans will not be driven out by a powerful political leader, there will be no revolution start date. For Jesus the kingdom of God is already here - it is among you, it is within you.

Luke's words are either translated as the kingdom of God is 'within you', or 'among you'. This leads us to two possible interpretations, both of which are true. The first is that the kingdom of God is within - Christ lives in us and the kingdom is within our hearts. We are co-creators of this kingdom with Christ, through our words and deeds, and the love we bring to birth in the world.

The second, more obvious explanation is that the kingdom of God is among you in the person of Jesus, preaching the Gospel of love and changing the hearts of those who listened to him. Both interpretations are true. Jesus was and is creating the kingdom, and it lies within the grasp of each of us. This is what Jesus meant when he said, 'Repent, for the kingdom of heaven is close at hand' (Matthew 4:17). In the 'Our Father' we pray 'thy kingdom come', asking for the vision to be able to know the God who is so close at hand in an intimate, personal way, and play our part in bringing his kingdom to fruition.

Instead of entering the kingdom of God when we die, by following Christ we become aware of heaven now. In the words of Thomas Merton, 'the gate of heaven is everywhere'. Heaven is here, and heaven is a community not an isolated experience. We live it together with our neighbours, and if we aren't prepared to love one another (and ourselves) then perhaps we aren't yet ready to experience the kingdom in the here and now.

This awareness always leads to action on behalf of others. There is no point recognising the great treasure that lies within, and keeping it locked in our hearts. The kingdom must be grown, the treasure must be shared, the fruits of the spirit must be passed on. In effect, Jesus is saying: repent, change, open your eyes - the kingdom is closer than you can ever imagine, and I need your help to make it grow.

....

> Do I believe that the kingdom of heaven is close
> at hand?

60

—

A Grain of Wheat

'unless a wheat grain falls on the ground and dies, it remains only a single grain; but if it dies, it yields a rich harvest. Anyone who loves his life loses it...'
(JOHN 12:24)

In the natural world, nothing lives unless something dies first. This is why Jesus teaches using nature (vines, fruit, wheat, birds), rather than flip charts full of theological propositions. The message is one of renewal or rebirth. If we are to follow him then part of us, like the grain of wheat, has to die. Jesus tells us that we have to die before we die; we must lose our life in order to find it.

What has to die is that part of us which is self-centred and self-obsessed - the powerful ego drive within us that constantly places our needs and wants above those of others. The ego is not 'emotionally intelligent', it is unconcerned with empathy and understanding - it's all about pride and self-advancement - Me, Myself and I. The ego does not want to die, but unless it does we cannot live.

Jesus tells us that we need to let go of something, so that something much bigger and better can replace it. This dying means losing some of the things that we think are essential to who we are. Our ego will object, it will tell us, 'You have spent your whole life becoming the person you are, why should you lose your attachments?' We are scared that if we let our defences down, if we let go of the safe and familiar, then our whole sense of who we are will disappear! We spend so long carefully creating our 'masks', cultivating our persona, our image, and we cling to it, as if it were who we truly are. Most of us are terrified of 'dying to self', but it has to be done. By all means read about this in Scripture and in theology books but at some point we all have to 'just do it'. It is only by 'doing it' that we understand it to be true.

This process of dying is *essential* because contained within the 'death' is the seed of our resurrection. As in nature, spring follows winter, life follows death. Jesus says, 'if anyone wants to be a follower of mine, let him renounce himself and take up his cross every day and follow me' (Luke 9:23-23). The whole point of 'taking up a cross' is not just to carry it, but to die on it.

Only then can we begin to bear much fruit, and 'yield a rich harvest'. St Paul describes it as giving us 'a new life'. When the ego dies then little or nothing can upset us - this is what Jesus describes as the 'peace the world cannot give'. For most of us this is an on-going journey rather than a one-off event, a slow evolution, a quiet 'giving up'. Being a Christian is about experiencing death and resurrection on a daily basis - when we go to work, do the washing up or help the children with their homework. And happily, the older we get the easier this process of letting go becomes.

Our little vision of who we are, based on our personal feelings and self-image is just not big enough or grand enough. It's too small and limiting, it fails to recognise the God within, it fails to understand that our true self is not something we acquire through 'blood, sweat and tears' - it's already there, 'hidden with Christ in God' (Colossians 3:3) - just waiting for us to wake up and see it. This is who we really are, everything else we think is important, our possessions and position in the world, will one day disappear, but this will live for ever.

The more we see Christ living in us, being part of us, then the more truly ourselves we become. Not I, but us - God living in me. And it doesn't stop there, it's never just God and me. It's always God and me and others.

....

What needs to die in me?

61

—

Suffering

Do not be afraid, for I have redeemed you; I
have called you by your name, you are mine.
Should you pass through the sea, I will be
with you; or through rivers, they will not
swallow you up.
(ISAIAH 43:1-2)

Suffering is part of life and for some it can weaken or destroy faith. Few of us go through life without pain or disappointment, but how we deal with such low moments is a choice each person makes, it is something within our control. When we see suffering as our teacher, then something can be learnt. God comes to us in our weakness, not in our self-regard and right-ness. If we look back at those 'hinge points' in our lives, those chapter endings and beginnings, those moments of personal change, we often find that they are accompanied by pain. Suffering makes us vulnerable; it helps destroy our inflated sense of ego and self-importance. It lowers our defences and makes us open to change, if we are willing to allow it. *However, if we don't allow our inner pain to transform us then we are liable to pass it on to others, and the circle of suffering continues.* Take a moment to read and ponder that last sentence again.

I remember being struck by a newspaper article about a person who became very sick with a life-changing illness. He said that he did not regret what had happened to him because his sickness had transformed his life; he had become a different person, less obsessed with himself and his own problems, more compassionate and empathetic, and more willing to risk love and appreciate the present moment. His suffering had become his teacher. By the grace of God he had seen a bigger picture and embraced a new perspective, which had, in a sense, 'saved him'.

We will all at some point have our own painful moment in the Garden of Gethsemane, but how we respond to it is very much a matter of choice - I can either allow it to sap my spirit, or I can see myself standing on holy ground. If we can see, in our suffering, our own vulnerability, our ultimate reliance on God and on his loving compassion, then we can transform the darkest situation into a route to salvation. In the gospels Jesus always travels to where the pain is – he sanctifies and makes holy everything he touches. He enables suffering to become holy because he himself suffered. Jesus on the cross tells us that when we are in pain - he is there too. We suffer *with* Christ, not for Him. Paul says, 'we suffer with him so that we may be glorified with him' (Romans 8:17). If we can unite our pain with the suffering of Jesus on the cross, we can through Him experience our own personal resurrection, and new life with Christ.

Recognising our own weakness and fragility is the starting point.

....

Can I see that difficulties and problems
might perhaps be essential elements of my
spiritual journey?

DOING CHRISTIANITY

62

—

Lord, Lord

'It is not those who say to me, "Lord, Lord", who will enter the kingdom of heaven but the person who does the will of my Father in heaven.'
(MATTHEW 7:21-22)

When I lived in the south of France I could see a mountain from my window, the Pic Saint- Loup. I decided to climb it one day - there were half a dozen paths to the top, some were steep and difficult, and others were gentle and winding, but took longer. I chose a gentle path and climbed up, inadvertently straying from the route occasionally, but always making it back, and pressing on. There were other people on other paths that day, but eventually I made it to the top, and so did they. We all arrived at the same place eventually. You could see for miles at the top, it was awe inspiring, one of those moments when you feel at one with nature, one with the Creator.

There is only one God, and we are all his children. When a Christian or a Muslim or a Hindu or a Jew or an atheist prays, the same God 'listens'. We may pray in different languages, and use different words, but there is only one God to hear our prayers. The mountain I climbed looked different if you stood north of it compared to the view from the south side. It *looked* different but was the same. My experience of climbing to the top was different to those on other paths but we all ended up in the same place.

We can sometimes believe that our view is the only view, that our experience is the only valid one, that our denomination is somehow superior to other ways. The need to belong to a group is an important human drive and much organised religion plays on this: are you 'saved', part of the 'chosen people', the 'elect', a member of the One True Holy Apostolic Church? All religions tend to believe that they are the ones that God likes best! But Jesus wasn't interested in tribal religion, God has no favourites - we are all loved and cherished equally. When Mother Teresa was asked if she attempted to convert people she answered, 'Yes I convert. I convert you to be a better Hindu, a better Christian, a better Catholic, a better Sikh, a better Muslim. When you have found God, it's up to you to do with him what you want.'

Jesus himself of course was a Jew. Christianity, the religion about him, would come later. Jesus doesn't seem to care too much for labels. He says that it is what is in a man's heart that matters, and how this is translated into loving actions, in order that 'the will of my Father in heaven' might be done.

....

Do I think less of others because their journey is different to mine?

63

Casting the first stone

'If there is one of you who has not sinned, let him be the first to throw a stone ...'
(JOHN 8:7)

The scribes and Pharisees brought to Jesus a woman who had been caught committing adultery; the punishment in the law for this was death by stoning. When Jesus challenges the Pharisees, 'If there is one of you who has not sinned, let him be the first to throw a stone', they disappear one by one. 'I do not condemn you' says Jesus to the woman, and he instructs her to 'go away and sin no more'. Notice that Jesus' disapproval is directed not so much at the woman who has sinned, but at those who think they are without sin.

It is easy to judge others. We do it all the time. We judge people on their appearance, their morality, their lifestyle, their social or ethnic background. Often that judgement is a negative one, a judgement of disapproval or in some cases contempt. We 'big ourselves up' by putting others down. As Fulton J Sheen put it, 'We think we make the picture hang straight on our wall by telling our neighbour that all his pictures are crooked.' Judgmentalism is at the heart of most gossip and idle chatter (often online these days), and most of us have experienced the negative consequences when this judgement is directed towards us. What a massive waste of time and energy.

Jesus doesn't just want to teach us, he wants to change us. He wants us to examine our own hearts rather than point the finger at others. An encounter with Jesus is always an invitation to see things differently, to change some aspect of our behaviour. For the Pharisees this change was about each of them accepting, one by one, that they too were sinners - they were not so 'high and mighty' after all, and far from perfect. The woman is rescued from certain death and receives a compassionate acceptance from Jesus, which must have led her to radically re-evaluate her life.

We are often trapped by our own sinfulness. But God is not keeping a record of our sins like a teacher with a mark book - he is waiting for an opportunity to forgive us. Realising that Jesus accepts us and forgives us, even when sometimes we condemn ourselves, is a powerful message of healing.

Jesus instructs the woman to 'sin no more'. This is almost impossible of course. We all do things we shouldn't do, and Jesus knows this. The point is to try as best we can to live a good life and turn away from wrongdoing, secure in the knowledge that Jesus stands ready to catch us each time we fall.

Hardly anyone consciously chooses to do evil. People do wicked things because they are unaware, because they lack consciousness, because they can't see the truth. The good news is that God uses our sinfulness, our failure, to bring us into the light. Like St Paul travelling on the road to Damascus to persecute Christians, we often need to be thrown from our horse and experience the resulting darkness and pain so that we can in time, turn towards and see the Light.

In what way do I need to stop judging others? Is there anyone in my family or friendship group that needs acceptance rather than condemnation?

64
—
Stewardship

*'The man who had received the five talents
promptly went and traded with them and
made five more.'*
(MATTHEW 25:16-17)

I once watched a TV programme called 'Making Slough
Happy', an attempt to discover the secrets of happiness in an ordinary British town. After much research a
Happiness Manifesto was produced, 'Ten Commandments
for Happiness' if you like! At number four was 'plant something', perhaps a window box or a pot plant, 'and keep it
alive'. The idea being that looking after something, nurturing
it, growing it, gives us a sense of achievement and satisfac-
tion. Humans like taking care of things - we like stewardship.

Understanding the concept of Christian stewardship
can, of itself, be life changing. If God created the universe
and everything in it, then we are entrusted to look after the
earth and all it contains. We are co-creators and collabo-
rators with him in the work of protecting, nurturing and
sanctifying our world. The planet and all its peoples and
resources are not to be exploited for short-term profit, all is
precious; our whole ecosystem is connected and we all play
a part in its protection.

If we accept this new way of seeing the world then our attitude to possessions and money changes. We do not really own things, we are simply temporarily in possession of certain items or money, and when we die they will all go to someone else. Hence, our duty is to see such things as gifts from God, and use them wisely (while we still can) for the benefit not just of ourselves, but for others too.

The same can be said of our talents and abilities. Perhaps God has gifted you with intelligence, wisdom, good looks, common sense, great strength or business acumen? The question is, will you use these gifts for the benefit of all, to make the world a better place, or will you simply use them to fuel your ego and satisfy your own personal desires? Like your possessions, your talents and skills will fade and disappear altogether one day - how will you account for your stewardship of these abilities?

We are also stewards of other people. Our children are gifts from God, they do not belong to us. We nurture and look after them for a while, but we don't own them. Our task is to give them 'roots and wings' and one day we will leave them, and they will remain for a while longer, perhaps to steward their own children. We are also stewards for our friends and others we encounter. Every interaction with another is an opportunity for us to 'steward', to look after, to nurture. We don't own others, and friends will come in and out of our lives, but we do have a duty to care for them, encourage them and love them.

Finally, we are stewards of our environment - the animals and plants, the sea and the sky. We inhabit our planet for a short while, and then pass it on to the next generation. We either selfishly exploit the natural world to temporarily enrich ourselves, or we ensure its survival for future generations. There is a forest on the coast in North Norfolk that I love to walk in. The trees were planted over 100 years ago by an enlightened landowner who has long since passed away and who never got to see the full fruits of his hard work, but the hundreds of trees he planted and nurtured have now grown into an awe-inspiring forest which sustains a rich variety of wildlife and gives pleasure to all who walk there. I wonder if he realised what a legacy he was leaving to future generations when he planted those initial saplings?

In the parable of the talents Jesus tells of a master who entrusts his money (or talents) to his servants. Two of them put their talents to work and multiply them, producing much fruit, but one servant who is afraid of the master just buries his - he does nothing to increase the gift he has been given, he goes for the safe option.

Jesus is asking us to use our God-given talents in his service rather than just sit on them. If we see God as generous and forgiving, then we, like the first two servants, will be ready to take risks to spread our gifts in the service of others. However, if we view God as a harsh and unforgiving master then we are likely to be less generous in our sharing and loving.

Of course the greatest gift we possess is the love God has given us, a love that grows by being given away. St Augustine urges us to 'Love and do what you will'. We are stewards of this love and every day is another opportunity to be generous and inclusive. My time on planet earth will one day come to an end, my time to love is now.

....

What legacy will I leave for future generations
- am I a faithful steward of the gifts I have been
given?

65

—

Gospel Comedy?

*The disciples had forgotten to take any food and
they had only one loaf with them in the boat.
Then he gave them this warning, 'Keep your eyes
open; be on your guard against the yeast of the
Pharisees and the yeast of Herod'. And they said
to one another, 'It is because we have no bread'.*
(MARK 8:14-17)

We often fail to see the bigger picture, and our cherished beliefs and ideas can get in the way of our search for a deeper truth. I once read a story (perhaps apocryphal) about a sit-down protest in Mexico at the famous Shrine of Our Lady of Guadalupe. The demonstrators were incensed that the local bishop had declared *Our Lady of Lourdes* patroness of the diocese - they were convinced that Our Lady of Guadalupe would be most offended by this terrible slight!

If the makers of Monty Python or Fawlty Towers were making a sketch out of a gospel scene then they may well start with the extract from Mark 8 above. The Pharisees had been annoying Jesus and he leaves them and gets in a boat with his disciples, who then realise they only have one loaf for the journey. Jesus wants to warn them about the legalistic, narrow-minded teachings of the Pharisees, but the disciples think he is worried about lunch. This is when Jesus perhaps has his John Cleese moment! Mark records Christ saying: 'Why are you talking about having no bread? Do you not understand? Have you no perception? Are your minds closed? Have you eyes that do not see, ears that do not hear?' He reminds the disciples that he fed the five thousand, so lunch won't be a problem!

As is so often the case, he is talking in metaphor - yeast is a substance that makes bread rise, it makes it appear larger, it fills it full of air. The teachings of the Pharisees and Herod appear 'delicious' to the onlooker but when you slice into their 'loaf' you realise that there is not as much there as you originally thought, and your hunger is not satisfied.

There is a serious point here and it concerns the dangers of literalism. The disciples think about food when Jesus wants to teach about truth. If we are not careful we can end up reading scripture, but not understanding. So much of what Jesus teaches is metaphor. He knows that it is impossible to put into black and white human language some of the mysteries of the kingdom of God, so he encourages us to see beyond the ordinary, to understand the truth behind the words. Scripture is often more poetry and metaphor than instruction manual. If we read any scripture as if it is merely a book of instructions then we can end up with religious fundamentalism; we just decide that we won't eat the Pharisee bread rather than shunning their teachings. We end up seeing but not understanding.

The words are not the truth, they only point away from ourselves to a greater truth beyond.

Can I see the truth beyond the words?

66

—

Temptation

*Filled with the Holy Spirit, Jesus left the Jordan
and was led by the Spirit through the wilderness,
being tempted there by the devil for forty days.*
(LUKE 4:1-2)

We all have our weaknesses, those areas of life which are hard to control, when we know we should be doing X but end up doing Y. In the prayer Jesus taught, we say 'lead us not into temptation, but deliver us from evil.' However, temptation is part of the human condition, and Jesus, being fully human, experienced temptation like everyone else.

Before Jesus starts his public ministry he goes into the desert to fast and pray for forty days. In fact Mark tells us that 'the Spirit drove him out into the wilderness', suggesting that like us, Jesus was reluctant to go, reluctant to confront the demons we all have to grapple with.

During this time he is tempted in the same ways that we are. Jesus gets hungry, and is tempted to turn stones into loaves. Like all temptations this appears at first glance to be rather beneficial (we rarely consider doing something which would appear to be harmful to us!). This bread however represents all the worldly possessions we are tempted to worship, not just fine food and wine but money, houses, cars - consumer goods we crave and desire because we think they will satisfy our inner hunger. Moreover, turning the stones into bread would have shown a lack of trust in the Father. Jesus knows that the Father will always provide him, and us, with everything we need.

Then Jesus is tempted by power and status. He is shown all the kingdoms of the world and knows that all of these can be his. He can become the 'King of the World' with all the attendant prestige, celebrity and worldly adulation; he literally has the world at his feet, if he wants it. Jesus was tempted here to turn away from his vocation, from the divine mission he had come to bring to fruition.

But Jesus recognises that these are false gods, saying 'You must worship the Lord your God and serve him alone.' He knows you can't worship two gods. And yet so often we profess to serve God whilst also pursuing money, power and position in society. Our pride and ego tell us that happiness is there for the taking, if only we had a bigger house or a better paying job or a bit more status and power. As a follower of Jesus we will often be tempted to go down a different path, to take the easy way, to 'put ourselves first for a change.' St. Augustine, as a young man, is reported to have prayed, 'Lord, make me pure - but not yet.'

To follow Christ is to see things in a new light, to see the temptations of false idols not as gateways to happiness, but as chains that enslave us. Jesus shows us how it's done in the desert. He rejects the temptations as a man, using his human will rather than any divine powers, showing us an example that we can follow. He chooses the narrow path, the way that leads to real freedom, and a peace that the world (with all its riches and kingdoms) can never give.

What are the biggest temptations in my life?

67

—

The Road to Emmaus

Now while he was with them he took the bread and said the blessing then he broke it and handed it to them and their eyes were opened and they recognised him but he had vanished from their sight.

(LUKE 24:30-32)

After Jesus' resurrection he appears alongside two disciples on the road to Emmaus. They do not recognise him, and they tell him of their disappointment at how things have turned out, how all their hopes have been dashed. It was only during their evening meal together at the breaking of bread that they recognised him. Later they said to each other, 'Did not our hearts burn within us as he talked to us on the road and explained the scriptures to us?'

Often our lives are frustrating and we think ourselves hard done by, like the two disciples on the road to Emmaus. It is easy to be discouraged sometimes. Perhaps your faith has gone stale, maybe you no longer pray as much as you did, perhaps you have stopped going to church on a regular basis. Or maybe you are sad because God seems distant, further away than perhaps he once was? Like the two disciples we often walk away from God, without realising that he is walking the road with us - we fail to recognise him when he is by our side. At such moments, like the Emmaus walkers, he listens to our complaints and frustrations, and if we listen to him, he shines a light on our problems. Perhaps our heart can burn a little as it did for the two disciples.

Allowing Christ in, enables us to see things from a different perspective - like the resurrection experience, perceived failure can be turned into triumph. During their evening meal when Jesus breaks the bread and shares it with them the disciples' eyes are opened, and they see him as he really is - the Eternal Christ, who was, and is, and is to come, the one about whom John says, 'Through him all things came to be'. He appears no longer as the 'historical Jesus' but as 'the Christ', who Matthew says lives, largely unnoticed, in the hungry, the thirsty, the stranger and the prisoner (Matthew 25:44-45).

We too can meet Christ in strange, unexpected places and fail to recognise him - we can ignore him, pass by on the other side, or worse still treat him unkindly.

Filled with a new found hope, the two disciples return to Jerusalem to tell the others - they have experienced their own resurrection moment - everything has changed, and they have work to do. The way the disciples are so utterly transformed after Jesus' death is perhaps the best evidence we have for the truth of the resurrection. This is important - any encounter with Christ is never an end in itself, it is an invitation to go out and make the world a more beautiful place.

Notice that only one of the two Emmaus walkers is mentioned - Cleopas. Luke does not name the other one. Perhaps we are the other one. Everyone who has felt downhearted about their faith, everyone who feels that things have turned out in ways they hadn't envisaged, or those who feel that life is a disappointment. Like the Emmaus walkers we need to listen to Christ gently whispering in our ear the truths of the Gospel. This can then give us the power to walk the road with others, those who need a listening ear, and be the face of Christ to those in need. If every road on life's journey is the road to Emmaus then we too will meet fellow travellers in need of our help and our words of encouragement.

Cleopas and the other disciple invited the stranger in at the end of the walk: *he made as if to go on; but they pressed him to stay with them. 'It is nearly evening' they said 'and the day is almost over'. So he went in to stay with them.*

....

Imagine that you are the other Emmaus walker and invite the risen Christ to stay with you awhile.

68

—

Seek and you will find

'Search and you will find; knock, and the door
will be opened to you.'
(MATTHEW 7:7-8)

What is it that is preventing you from following Christ more faithfully? Are you afraid that he will make demands on you that you cannot go along with? Changes to your life that will be disruptive and lead to unhappiness perhaps? Do you think that you are not worthy of God's friendship because of things you have done in the past? Are you stuck in a cosy routine, a way of thinking and living that you are afraid to challenge or disturb? Do you want to keep God at a distance, keeping things as they are - God is something for an hour on Sunday perhaps but no more? Are you unsure whether any of it is really true, or whether it really will lead to 'living life to the full?' Are you so busy that you feel there is little time in your day to ponder the big questions of life - 'why are we here' and 'what's the point of everything?' Have you had negative experiences of church which have made you disillusioned with organised religion? Have you been turned off by the attitude of the clergy or the behaviour of other Christians? Has past sadness, disappointment or tragedy left you feeling hostile towards God?

If you are asking these questions then you have already chosen the right path. Our life is a pilgrimage, a journey where we search for meaning, question everything, seek something better and strive to be the best version of ourselves. If we are asking questions and looking for answers then we are halfway there. Holman Hunt's painting, 'The Light of the World', shows Christ standing outside the door of our house, knocking patiently, holding a light. The door has no handle on the outside. Whoever is on the inside must open the door; a door covered in ivy which has never been opened before. The search is over when we open that door from the inside and realise that God has been there all the time, waiting for us. The one who searches will always find - and finding God is rarely a 'thunderbolt moment', but a quiet and calm acceptance and realisation that I am loved, and that is enough, and all will be well. The Gospel of Jesus tells us that our life is not so much about reaching out to find God, but about God reaching out to find us. God does not withhold himself from us, but we withhold ourselves from him. Finding him is really allowing him to find us.

Am I prepared to open the door?

STEP FIVE

A New Way of Doing

*Show me your faith without works, and I by
my works will show you my faith...*
(JAMES 2:18)

When I was a teacher I worked alongside Mr Hill, a committed Christian who was well liked by staff and students because he treated everyone with respect and kindness. Many of our pupils were Muslim and I often enjoyed discussing faith matters with them. One of my students, Ali, once said to me, 'I often tell my friends, if you want to know how to be a good Muslim, look at Mr Hill'. At the age of seventeen Ali had understood a profound truth about religion – it is less about what you believe and more about what you do. Mr Hill knew little about Islam, but in another sense, he knew everything. We reveal our faith in God by what we do rather than what we think, or in the words of the Church Father, Maximus the Confessor: 'faith is made manifest in action.'

Step Four was about seeing things in a different light, changing our perspective. But seeing things in a new light means little if it doesn't change the way we do things. It's rarely our thinking that cause us to change; rather it's our loving actions that cause us to think differently.

Few homilies in church lead to personal transformation. Almost all spiritual knowledge we have comes through *participation*. We can only find out if something is true by doing it. In the extracts that follow Jesus makes it clear that actions speak louder than words or thoughts. Mental belief systems are all about religion – faith, on the other hand, is about spirituality. It takes us to different places and asks us to change. In this crucial Fifth Step Jesus shows us how to replace *orthodoxy* (right beliefs) with *orthopraxy* (right practice) - religion is not primarily about what you understand, but about what you do. In other words, we 'do' Christianity rather than believe in it (our faith is a verb, not a noun). Reality or 'truth' is about how we live our life rather than the ideas we believe in – in the words of James, 'If good works do not accompany faith, it is quite dead' (James 2:14).

And our small actions have a ripple effect, like a stone tossed in a pond. The good we do, however small, sets off a chain reaction for others, helping us to share in Christ's work of making 'thy kingdom come on earth as it is in heaven.'

69

—

Know them by their fruits

'You will know them by their fruits.'
(MATTHEW 7:16)

ating five portions of fruit and vegetables each day is supposed to improve our health. Jesus often refers to seeds and crops in the Gospel, and there are thirty two references to fruit in the New Testament! And Jesus says - you will know what kind of person someone is, by the fruits they produce. John records Jesus saying: 'the works my Father has given me to carry out, these same works of mine testify that the Father has sent me' (John 5:36).

This highlights the important truth that is at the very heart of the Gospel message – *religion is not primarily about what you believe, it is about what you do*. Marcus Borg lays it out clearly: 'You can believe all the right things and still be a jerk. You can believe all the right things and still be miserable. Faith as believing, that is, believing with our head, is really pretty impotent'. It is no good having a wonderfully coherent set of theological principles in our heads, if our hearts are made of stone, and if our beliefs do not bear fruit in our daily 'works' or actions. Jesus commissions us 'to go out and to bear fruit, fruit that will last'. It is not our intellectually correct theology or our charismatic personality that makes us holy; it is what we do - practical everyday actions, that help others and make the Kingdom of God a reality. It's easy to say 'I believe' or 'I'm a Christian' - the hard bit is 'the doing': forgiving others, loving the unloved and building up the community.

It is almost always our actions and experiences that create a new set of beliefs in our head rather than the other way round.

In time our tiny seed can grow to become 'a mustard tree', sheltering others in its branches and extending hope and friendship to those around us. According to St Ignatius, 'love is shown more in deeds than words.' Love is not simply a feeling or a good intention - it exists only in the sense that it is demonstrated. You might imagine that you are loving, but unless you love another, this is just an idea in your head. You may think you are generous, but unless this is manifested in actual giving then it is just a thought about who you think you are.

It is not enough to say 'Lord, Lord', to say 'Jesus is Lord'. Perhaps we see ourselves in the 'God-fearing Christian' who goes to church each Sunday and then fails to lift a finger to help a needy neighbour? We are called to be an adult, to take full responsibility for what we say and do and think. As Dietrich Bonhoeffer said, 'Your life as a Christian should make non-believers question their disbelief in God.'

Christianity is about doing stuff. You cannot be a 'theoretical Christian' - to be a Christian means to put into practice the teaching of Christ. That's the only test. We worship God by what we do: 'My children, our love is not to be just words or mere talk, but something real and active; only by this can we be certain that we are children of the truth' (1 John 3:18-19).

Moreover, we don't do good things because we want to be rewarded with a free pass into heaven. We 'do good' to create the kingdom of heaven here and now; goodness is its own reward.

Jesus says it is not necessarily those who say 'Lord, Lord' who will find favour in his eyes but those who do 'the will of my Father in heaven'. Yes, actions really do speak louder than words.

....

How can I make my faith real through what I do each day?

70

—

The Good Samaritan

'who is my neighbour?'
(LUKE 10:29-30)

Lawyers are good at asking difficult questions, and one asks Jesus what he needs to do to 'inherit eternal life?' Jesus, like any good teacher, asks *him* what he thinks he needs to do. The lawyer replies - 'you must love the Lord your God with all your heart ... and your neighbour as yourself'. Jesus praises the answer and says, 'do this and life is yours'. But this is not enough for the lawyer and he replies with, 'And who is my neighbour?' This may seem obvious, but in asking this question the lawyer is trying to get Jesus to identify who is *not* his neighbour - he wants to know who he doesn't need to love!

This leads Jesus to tell perhaps the greatest, most famous parable of all - the Good Samaritan. It is the gospel in a nutshell.

Whilst the priest and Levite pass by on the other side of the road, the Samaritan helps the injured man. Maybe the priest and the Levite looked at the man and felt sorry for him; perhaps the thought to help him did cross their minds? But thoughts don't bandage the man's wounds or carry him to safety. It was the *actions* of the Samaritan that made the difference. Jesus chooses of course to have a Samaritan rescue the man - a person most of his listeners would have despised.

Jesus provides great detail in this story about exactly how the Samaritan treats the injured man, focusing on his kindness and generosity, and the way he involves others (the innkeeper) in caring for the man (we're better when we work together). At the end of the story Jesus turns the lawyer's original question on its head, not: 'Who is my neighbour?' but 'What kind of neighbour am I?' or 'How can I be a good Samaritan for others?'

'That's nothing to do with me' and 'don't get involved' are phrases we hear all too often. 'Walking by on the other side' has become for many a way of life. The Samaritan however, just responds to need - he doesn't care who he is helping, he responds with mercy, no questions asked. Jesus ends the parable with the simple instruction to humanity, 'Go, and do the same yourself'.

Identifying who we are in this parable is an interesting exercise. We might end up thinking that we are the priest or the Levite. We might believe in God, know our Ten Commandments, say our prayers, go to church and sponsor friends running marathons for charity. We've heard this parable a hundred times, we are familiar with the theory and the theology. We profess to 'know' Christ, but we have made our God so small that we can't see him when he's lying battered and bruised at the roadside... so we walk on by.

We can also look at the parable in another way. We can see ourselves as the wounded person lying in the road. Various people and 'ways of thinking' pass us by, but Christ is the Good Samaritan, sent by the Father to bind our wounds, take us to a place of safety and restore us from death to life.

....

Where do I see myself in this parable?

71

—

The Two Sons

*'I tell you solemnly, tax collectors and
prostitutes are making their way into the
kingdom of God before you.'*
(MATTHEW 21:31)

Politicians love to win votes by ingratiating themselves
with their audience, often saying whatever they think
the people want to hear. If Jesus was standing for election it would be hard to see him getting many votes when he
addressed the words above to the chief priests and elders.
Jesus spoke truth to power. He was not seeking popularity,
he just wanted people to change, and stay changed.

Jesus tells the chief priests and elders a parable about a man
with two sons. He asks the first to go and work in his vineyard
- the boy refuses, then thinks better of it, and goes. The second
son says, 'Certainly sir', when asked to work, but then decides
not to go. Jesus invites his listeners to compare themselves with
those who outwardly profess to be faithful followers of God, but
in their behaviour and lifestyle refuse to believe the truth, even
when they are shown 'a pattern of true righteousness'.

Here is Jesus emphasising one of the most important themes
of the Gospel. He is on the side of the son whose actions are
good even though he says the wrong thing, as opposed to the
son who says all the right things and then does nothing.

It is interesting how Jesus' teaching resonates so deeply with the tax collectors and prostitutes. They were on the margins of society and so much more open to Jesus' message of loving inclusion in God's family. When we can acknowledge our sinfulness, our egotism, our half-heartedness and unworthiness, our need of God, then we are much more open to the possibility of radical permanent change. You could say we all need to become more like tax collectors and prostitutes!

The chief priests and the elders, on the other hand, have positions of power and status, they have wealth and prestige; they have so much worldly stuff to lose by following Jesus. And they just can't see their own pride, self-righteousness and pomposity - they lack the self-awareness to understand that they are at the back of 'God's queue'.

Perhaps some of them ended up paying lip service to Jesus, perhaps the best of them could see in their hearts that his message was true - but they had so much invested in the status quo that any sort of real change in their inner selves was incredibly difficult. If we are not careful we can end up demonizing the elders and priests instead of reflecting on how similar they are in many ways to those of us who say 'Yes, certainly' to Christ, saying all the right words in the right order in our prayers and worship, but then deciding not to turn up for work in the vineyard.

Jesus is a realist. He knows that there are aspects of following him which will be difficult for us. He knows our initial response, like the first son, might be to say 'no, I will not go'. Of course we are free to do that, but Jesus hopes that in the end we will trust him enough to put in our daily shift in the vineyard, and in doing so find our life's work and vocation.

Am I ready to do my shift?

72

—

Forgiveness

'Lord, how often must I forgive my brother if he wrongs me? As often as seven times?' Jesus answered 'Not seven, I tell you, but seventy-seven times.'
(MATTHEW 18:21-22)

A little boy was praying, asking God to bless each of his family members, but left out his brother. 'Why didn't you pray for Sam?' said his Mum. The boy replied, 'Because he hit me'. Mum said, 'Don't you remember, Jesus said to forgive your enemies?' And the little boy replied 'Exactly! He's not my enemy, he's my brother!'

It's great to be forgiven – we expect it from others. But we find it difficult to forgive, and sometimes refuse to do it, often to those closest to us. In such cases we might need to think about self-forgiveness. If we are unable to forgive ourselves then we will find it difficult to forgive others, indeed we are likely to pass our pain on to them.

However, forgiving our neighbour is a non-negotiable pillar of the gospel, and is absolutely essential if we are to follow Christ. It has been estimated that over half of all Jesus' teaching relates in one way or another to forgiveness.

We hurt ourselves by failing to forgive. It hardens our hearts; turns them into 'hearts of stone' and makes us bitter and resentful. Whatever you do to someone else, you do to

DOING CHRISTIANITY

yourself. By loving another you are loving and taking care of yourself and when you forgive another you forgive yourself. Everything is circular, everything is connected. Eastern religions might say 'what goes around comes around' or as St Paul put it in Galatians 'as you sow so shall you reap'.

A lack of forgiveness means that we keep our focus on the past rather than living in the present and looking to the future. Holding on to grudges simply fuels our anger and eats away at our tranquillity. In the words of Corrie Ten Boom, 'Forgiveness is setting the prisoner free, only to find out that the prisoner was me'. When we forgive we can start the healing process, both within ourselves and of course in the one who has been forgiven. Forgiving a person extends to them the opportunity to change and grow. Jesus wants us to forgive unconditionally, and to have no limit to our forgiveness (more than seventy-seven times if needs be). We who have been forgiven by God must now extend that grace to each other. As Daniel O'Leary said 'Heaven is on earth when a person forgives'.

Most hurts we receive are unintentional - the other person didn't intend to upset us - and these are easier to forgive. However, many people have suffered terrible wrongs in the past at the hands of others. In such cases it is possible to forgive the person whilst condemning the action. Hence forgiveness is not a *forgetfulness* of the past; it is to risk a new future other than the one imposed by the past or by its memory. In short forgiveness sets us free, allows us to move on and enables us, in turn, to be forgiven. For how can we expect to be forgiven ourselves if we are not prepared to extend the healing power of forgiveness to others.

Are there people I need to forgive now? What is a failure to forgive, doing to me?

73

—

Humility

*'Anyone who exalts himself will be humbled, and
anyone who humbles himself will be exalted.'*
(MATTHEW 23:11-12)

Humility has been called the mother of all virtues but is also perhaps the hardest to acquire. When I asked a friend what his New Year's resolution was, he said, 'I'm going to be more humble... which should be easy as I'm already really good at it!'

Our politicians, business leaders and entertainment stars often find humility difficult, perhaps because the world so often presents arrogance as strength, and humility as weakness. Jesus' strength of course comes from his humility and powerlessness (hence the title Lamb of God).

Pope Francis says: 'This is God's way, the way of humility. It is the way of Jesus; there is no other. And there can be no humility without humiliation'. What Pope Francis is saying is that we need to recognise how the bubble of our self-importance needs to be pricked, we need to understand how humiliation is essential, and we must accept it, and even welcome it. One could almost say 'give us this day our daily humiliation!' Such a practice might appear to leave us powerless, but it actually grants us enormous spiritual strength.

So what does being humble mean in practice? If we are

humble we realise that we don't know everything, and we never will. This means accepting that I will often be wrong. If all men and women are of equal value (in God's eyes no one is better or worse than I am) then there is no need to judge others in order to boost my own self-esteem. It means we will see conversation less about listing our own magnificent achievements, and more about making the other feel good about themselves. We will refrain from being defensive and we let go of the idea that we always have to be right. If we are humble we will express gratitude for the gift of life we have been given - this makes us less inclined to see ourselves as the centre of the universe, and more willing to focus on those around us. Humble people are good at conveying gratitude to others.

Humility is not about thinking less of yourself – it is thinking of yourself less. If we can see ourselves as God sees us, then we will have no problems with self-worth and self-esteem, and there will be no need to 'big ourselves up'. We will have the quiet confidence that comes from knowing that we are forever in the loving gaze of our Creator. We must embrace our humanity - we know we will make mistakes, we will sin, we will do stupid things, but we are secure in the knowledge that God's forgiveness is never-ending. As Pope Francis says, 'Let Jesus preach to you, and let Jesus heal you. We are all wounded. Everyone.' Like the prodigal son there is always a banquet awaiting us when we turn with humility to our Father in heaven.

In Micah 6:8 we read perhaps a perfect summation of the whole Gospel message: 'This is what Yahweh asks of you: only this, to act justly, to love tenderly and to walk *humbly* with your God'.

....

How can I embrace and welcome humility into my life?

74
—
Losing your life

'Anyone who wants to save his life will lose it;
but anyone who loses his life for my sake, that
man will save it. What gain, then, is it for a
man to have won the whole world and to have
lost or ruined his very self?'
(Luke 9:24-26)

We are all on a journey - a physical journey from birth to death, and a spiritual journey from death to life.

I wonder what people will say about us when we are gone? The answer of course will depend on our actions, what we have done, and the goals we pursued. Thomas Merton said, 'If you have learned only how to be a success, your life has probably been wasted'. Did our life revolve around 'success' at work at the expense of our relationships? Was our priority amassing nice possessions, or making money? Did we spend our time seeking personal pleasure for ourselves without consideration of those in need, whether close at hand or far away? Did we live life without any thought of the environmental damage we were inflicting on the planet for future generations? Jesus tells us 'what good will it be for someone to gain the whole world, yet lose their soul?' There is little point in pursuing wealth or career if we end up losing our soul (notice that Jesus never once mentions the importance of having 'a good career' in the Gospel).

So how do we save our life? Jesus tells us we must lose our attachment to the material things of this world (things the media often tells us are essential for our happiness). We can own material things of course, but we shouldn't 'worship' them - they are not the point of life. To 'gain' your life is to stop thinking that your happiness depends on 'stuff'. By dying to self, and dying to our worldly attachments, we provide the space in our hearts to think of others and pursue goals which are not driven by our own self-interest.

Our modern Western consumer-oriented view of the world is essentially about *taking* - what can I get out of a given situation, what can I acquire - and we measure success by how much we've got. The gospel of Jesus is primarily about *giving not getting* - giving away your time, your love, your money - giving yourself to others, giving yourself to Christ. And paradoxically by giving away your life, you gain it.

It isn't that hard to profess belief in the Lord. But discipleship is much more than this, it is to enter through the 'narrow gate' and tread 'the narrow road that leads to life', and that is not so easy. It is a life-changing journey of continuous daily action not a one-off decision to believe something. But the rewards are worth the struggle. The promise of Jesus is there for all of us to seize hold of and make our own – 'whoever loses their life for me will find it'.

What things do I need to become less attached to in order to 'find' my life?

75

—

Non-violence

Then they came forward, seized Jesus and took him in charge. At that, one of the followers of Jesus grasped his sword and drew it; he struck out at the high priest's servant, and cut off his ear. Jesus then said, 'Put your sword back, for all who draw the sword will die by the sword.'
(MATTHEW 26:50-53)

It has been estimated that over 10% of all wars in history have had religion as their primary cause. The 11th century Crusades were recognised as a 'holy war', proclaimed and enthusiastically encouraged by popes, and declared as a penitential exercise that brought forgiveness of sins for those who joined. St Francis of Assisi however, opposed the Crusades, and travelled to Egypt to initiate dialogue with Muslim leaders.

Since time began humans have seen violence as inevitable, as the only way in which some problems can be solved. We can only defeat those who might wish to do us harm by employing stronger, greater violence from our side. This has been referred to as 'redemptive violence' - violence that will set us free from evil. Most religions teach the idea of a 'just war' and Christianity is no different. Both Augustine and

Aquinas outlined the criteria which would justify war. In recent times the leadership of the Russian Orthodox Church vigorously supported Putin's invasion of Ukraine, calling it a holy war. However Saint John XXIII pointed out, that in the modern era, 'it no longer makes sense to maintain that war is a fit instrument with which to repair the violation of justice'.

When we look at Jesus' actions and words we find non-violence at the centre. He tells his followers to love their enemies, to 'bless those who curse you', and if a person strikes you on one cheek, offer the other one as well. In the Sermon on the Mount he says 'blessed are the peacemakers for they shall be called sons of God'. Christ is insistent that his followers demonstrate love to all they encounter.

It can be argued that the moment you curse or condemn another you join them; you don't defeat violence by embracing it yourself. Violence repaid with violence just perpetuates the cycle, hence Jesus' words at his arrest: 'all who draw the sword will die by the sword'. It is hard to reconcile Christ's teaching with violence and war. In the 'Our Father' we ask God to 'deliver us from evil', but we appear to want to do that by placing our faith in our ever more sophisticated military hardware, rather than placing our trust in God. In the last century Gandhi was able to eventually achieve his objectives through nonviolence, but many doubt whether Hitler could have been defeated using similar methods. We will never know.

For Jesus the path of nonviolence ended in his death on the cross, a fate which often befalls those who oppose unjust political systems with non-violent resistance. Dietrich Bonhoeffer, a German Lutheran pastor and pacifist, preached opposition to Hitler through non-violent activism. In 1934 he urged all the churches to speak with one voice in a 'great ecumenical council' which would forbid war, 'take the weapons from the hands of their sons' and proclaim 'the peace of Christ against a raging world'. No such proclamation took place, there was no ecumenical council - the World War began five years later, and Bonhoeffer was hanged by the Nazis in 1945.

....

How can I be a peacemaker?

76

—

Imagine

*Glory be to him whose power, working in us, can
do infinitely more than we can ask or imagine;
glory be to him from generation to generation in
the Church and in Christ Jesus for ever and ever.*
(EPHESIANS 3:20-21)

I was listening to John Lennon's famous song 'Imagine'
on the radio. In it, he says 'Imagine there's no heaven,
it's easy if you try. No hell below us, above us only sky...
Nothing to kill or die for, and no religion too'.

It got me thinking. Imagine if the most important principle repeated day and night by all the churches was love.
Imagine if Christians visited those in prison, fed the hungry
and looked after widows and orphans. What if the homeless,
the down and outs and the disadvantaged were sought out
and given a welcome in our places of worship. Imagine if
the Churches divested themselves of most of their material
wealth and gave the money to the poor. Imagine if the Pope
lived in a small guest house with lots of other people, rather
than alone in the luxurious Vatican apartments (Pope Francis
does actually!) What if Christians were in the forefront of the
movement for environmental protection. Imagine if we could
all accept that we don't have all the answers all the time, and

that perhaps we could learn from other denominations, other faiths and those with no faith. Imagine if we were so at peace with ourselves, and so confident of our faith that we felt no need to harm anybody else. Imagine if we could be so compassionate that we could accept and welcome all God's children whatever their ethnicity, religion, gender or sexuality. What if no one was afraid of death or eternal damnation because they were so confident in the compassion and mercy of a God who loves them more than they could ever imagine.

If we could do all this, then the final line of John Lennon's 'Imagine' might come to pass - 'And the world will live as one'. Is all this impossible to imagine? Well as Jesus said, 'everything is possible for God'.

Can I imagine myself having a role in creating a different future for the world?

77

—

The Barren Fig Tree

'it may bear fruit next year...'
(LUKE 13:9).

I enjoy gardening but I'm not particularly patient - if a plant isn't thriving then I tend to dig it up and replace it with something else. Why should it take up space in my rockery if it's not going to flower?

Jesus tells the parable about a man with a fig tree in his vineyard which has not produced any fruit for three years. He tells his gardener to cut it down - it's just wasting space. But the gardener replies, 'leave it one more year and give me time to dig around it and manure it: it may bear fruit next year...'

Many of us are like the barren fig tree. We take up space, we bask in the sunshine and soak up the rainwater for ourselves, but give nothing back, produce no fruit for others to enjoy. Quite happy to potter along with no bigger purpose in life, just being, but not giving.

Followers of Jesus are expected to do stuff - produce fruit, give generously, help those in need, be compassionate and forgiving. These are the fruits of the Spirit. We take heart that Jesus is a patient gardener - he doesn't write us off, he is always ready to give us a second chance.

Imagine if we have another year to produce some fruits for Christ. Can we ask him to dig around us, to fertilize us with the Spirit, to encourage us to acts of kindness for others? What can we do in the year ahead to turn our barren fig tree into something beautiful for God, to repay the patient trust he has shown in us?

....

Our little fig tree will one day be no more and its ability to bear fruit will go with it. Let us not waste time, let us put our barren years behind us. Let us seize the opportunity whilst we still have time and see what fruit we can produce in the year ahead.

78

—

Unto dust you shall return

'This very night the demand will be made for your soul; and this hoard of yours, whose will it be then?'
(LUKE 12:20-21)

When I was a teacher I used to amuse my students by telling them with great vigour - 'You are all going to die!' This would always cause nervous laughter - most 16-year-olds never consider death, and certainly don't believe it will ever happen to them. In fact many of us *never* really consider it - and in modern Western societies it has become something of a taboo subject. However, talking and thinking about death can cause us to appreciate life more fully, to live life in the present. I remember visiting the National Gallery in London and finding various old paintings where the artist had included a skull, often in a portrait, or resting on a table. The artist wants to remind the viewer of their own mortality and the ultimate futility of vanity, and the pursuit of worldly riches or fame: 'remember man that you are dust and unto dust you shall return'. In times gone by, life was short and unpredictable - the paintings are telling the viewer, 'Death is coming, prepare yourself!'.

Jesus tells the disciples the parable of the 'rich fool'. The rich man spends his life storing his growing grain harvest in ever bigger barns, and then when they are full, says to himself, now I can 'take things easy, eat, drink and have a good time'. But that night he dies, and the treasure he stored up so painstakingly on earth will go to someone else or be left to rot.

Jesus asks us to make ourselves 'rich in the sight of God' for 'a man's life is not made secure by what he owns'. One day we will die, you and I, that is inevitable. So if you are going to store up treasure for yourself in heaven then get on with it. Do what you need to do now, tell those you love that you love them now, give generously to charity now, forgive those who need forgiving now, help others who need your help now. As St Francis of Assisi said, 'Remember that when you leave this earth, you can take with you nothing that you have received only what you have given: a full heart enriched by honest service, love, sacrifice and courage'.

To know and appreciate that death is coming jolts us out of complacency and shifts our focus to the now - 'stay awake', says Jesus, 'because you do not know either the day or the hour'. (Matthew 25:13).

Is there anything that I've been 'putting off' that I need to do now?

79

—

The Trial

'I have not come to call the righteous, but sinners.'
(MARK 2:17)

At school we used to have lessons in Religious Knowledge. We were taught about such things as the Ten Commandments, why a 'mortal sin' was very bad news, and lots of detail from the Catechism. We had to learn things by heart, and at the start of each lesson we would be quizzed about our knowledge from the previous day. If we got anything wrong we had to write out the answers again ten times, so as to make sure it was all imprinted on our memory. I used to avoid getting things wrong by writing out the correct answers on tiny pieces of paper and secreting them in my pencil case (which could be quickly zipped up if the teacher decided to go walkabout). Today, Religious Knowledge in school has been replaced by Religious Education, and thankfully things are much improved.

All this came to mind when I came across the question: 'If you were put on trial for being a Christian, would there be enough evidence to convict you?' Oh dear, I started to feel uncomfortable.

I began to wonder what the judge might be asking me. Well, they probably wouldn't want me to explain to the jury the doctrines of the Trinity or the Incarnation. I wouldn't be questioned about the tricky 'Problem of Evil', asked to name the Seven Deadly Sins, or recite the Creed from memory. The things I learnt at school would sadly be of no use to me here - there would be no need for the pencil case. My Religious Knowledge exam certificates would not be accepted as evidence. Neither would the judge be interested in whether I went to church on a Sunday or said my daily prayers.

I would most likely be asked: 'did you give something to eat when people were hungry? Did you give something to drink to those who were thirsty? Did you welcome the stranger? Did you look after the sick? Were you slow to judge others, and swift to bless? Did you use the gifts you had been given in the service of others? Did you quickly forgive, and did you stay generous and humble of heart? And then the most important question - did you love?

And then when it looked as if I would 'get off' all the charges and be proven not guilty of being a Christian, I imagined that Jesus might show up as the star witness. He would say that yes, I was very half-hearted in my approach, and that yes, I was a sinner. But he would also say that I was exactly the sort of person that he had come for, and how delighted he was to have me in his flock. His eloquence would win over the jury, and I would be convicted on all the charges.

80

—

Living the Faith

You have stripped off your old behaviour
with your old self, and you have put on a
new self which will progress towards true
knowledge the more it is renewed in the image
of its creator... There is only one Christ: he is
everything and he is in everything.
(Colossians 3:9-11)

One of the dominant themes of this book is that actions speak louder than words or beliefs. In the Gospel, all those who meet Jesus with an open heart are changed. The disciples didn't fall in love with a set of doctrines, they fell for Jesus, and that loving relationship changed how they behaved. Believing in a person is very different to believing that a set of principles about the person are true. Believing in someone requires trust and love; believing theological statements merely implies some form of intellectual assent.

In 1 John 2:9 we hear that, 'Anyone who claims to be in the light but hates his brother is still in the dark'. 'Claiming' is a *believing* word, a mental assent to an idea; 'hating' is *doing* – it's practical. In other words, claiming something counts for little – it is in the doing, in the loving, that we find the Light. Jesus says

'If you love me, you will keep my commandments'. We express our love for God by a practical programme of action.

If we decide to 'believe in' Christ then we should expect changes in our behaviour and habits to follow on from this choice. We might decide to go to church more often but this will not automatically make us a 'follower of Christ'.

Here are some if the changes that might flow from taking to heart the gospel message. As we begin to see Christ in others, we will understand that although certain people commit evil deeds, they are not of themselves evil. If we are prepared to look harder, we will see that Christ lives in the sinner as well as the saint. We will no longer seek to distance ourselves from the unloved, but want to stand shoulder to shoulder with those who are disadvantaged. We will pray differently - the shopping list of requests will be replaced with more silence, more quiet connection, more resting in God's presence, and more listening. As we look at the world differently, we will see God in all things and everyone, round every street corner and in every drop of rain. Our work will take on a different meaning - like St Therese we will find beauty and holiness in the most mundane of activities, 'finding God in the washing up', discovering the sacred in the ordinary. We will consume differently - deciding that we don't always need to wear the latest fashions if this means buying yet another cheap garment made in a sweatshop in a developing country.

You will find that you don't actually need so many pairs of shoes or items of clothing, and when you do need something, you will try to source it from a supplier that you know pays their workers a fair wage. Because you know that when you feed the hungry you are feeding Christ, you will give generously to charity. You may also decide to volunteer more; you will say yes, more often than no. Your faith may propel you to support various pressure groups which are fighting for social justice and equality. Paying your fair share of tax (rendering unto Caesar) will be a source of quiet pride rather than something you complain about, as you appreciate the need to contribute to the well-being of the wider community. If you invest in the stock market you will carefully consider the companies in your portfolio and divest yourself of those that don't fit with your new ethical framework. You will re-use and recycle more, and throw less away, as you understand the wonder and fragility of God's Creation. And most importantly you will take every opportunity to love more and to make others feel valued; seeing others not as objects that might benefit you in some way but brothers and sisters, co-creators of the kingdom of God on earth. Your new perspective then has a chance to ripple out to those you meet (even those people you don't like) and change them too. You will be free to be the person you were created to be; free to love, and to be loved.

If we aren't open to change, if we don't 'walk the walk', then we remain like those who heard the word of God, nodded to themselves and then went on their way.

....

Pick one thing from the list above and start doing it!

STEP SIX

A New Way of Giving

J ames tells the early followers of Christ that if one of them, "is in need of clothes and has not enough food to live on, and one of you says to them, 'I wish you well; keep warm and eat plenty', without giving them these bare necessities of life, then what good is that? Faith is like that: if good works do not go with it, it is quite dead" (James 2:15-17). Our Christian lives have to be about *giving* rather than *getting* – sadly many people never realise this until it's too late.

Jesus was the 'Servant King', and we are called to a life of service for others (and of course, how we relate to others is how we relate to God). In Step 6, Jesus shows us how we receive when we give, and how our lives take on meaning through our relationships with others.

81

—

Generosity

*'Give and there will be gifts for you: a full
measure, pressed down, shaken together, and
running over, will be poured into your lap;
because the amount you measure out is the
amount you will be given back.'*
(Luke 6:38)

The philosopher Peter Singer once posed an interesting ethical question: if you went past a small child drowning in a pond, would you jump in and pull her out even if it meant muddying your clothes? He then argued that if you'd do that, and almost everyone would, then you also have a responsibility to save someone in a faraway land who is dying of starvation (by giving to a charity working in the developing world). According to Singer, distance from the event should not be a factor for consideration - a lack of generosity towards those faraway is as bad as letting the child drown on your doorstep.

According to Oxfam almost half the world, over three billion people, live on less than $5.50 a day (just over £4). The planet's richest 1% own half of the world's wealth, and this figure is rising not falling (interestingly the super-rich also manage to avoid as much as 30% of their tax liability).

At the other end of the spectrum 70% of the world's population account for just 2.7% of global wealth. If you are reading this book and live in a developed country it is likely that you are amongst the wealthiest people that have ever lived.

Giving is an essential part of the Gospel message; Jesus demands generosity from his followers. He praises the widow who contributes 'all she had to live on' to the treasury when the rich gave only what 'money they had over'. Mother Teresa said, 'if you give what you do not need, it isn't giving'. St Paul urges the early Christians to 'give cheerfully', and there is a strong tradition in Christianity of giving a tithe, a percentage of one's income, to charity.

In the *Summa Theologiae*, St Thomas Aquinas promotes a vision of generosity that is radical and challenging. He quotes St Ambrose as follows: 'feed him that is dying of hunger; if you have not fed him, you have slain him... the bread that you withhold belongs to the hungry; the clothing that you store away belongs to the naked; and the money that you bury in the earth is the redemption and security of the penniless.'

The Gospel instruction to be generous does not just refer to charitable giving. Giving to others through our acts of kindness and love, or through generous giving of our time or our care will be reflected back to us. In other words, it is not just the receiver who benefits from our good actions but we the giver too. In other passages in the Gospel Jesus refers to reaping what we sow. We are urged to be people who give, people who serve, for it is in giving that we receive. Our generosity is a reflection of God's generosity to us. It is giving back to him what he has first given to us.

One of my favourite charities is Mary's Meals. Non-denominational they aim to provide a daily meal in school for children in some of the poorest countries in the world. This encourages children to go to school each day and receive an education which for many is a way out of poverty. It costs £16 to feed a child for a whole school year (www.marysmeals.org.uk).

82

—

How to Be Happy

A palliative care nurse, Bonnie Ware, wrote down the most common regrets of her dying patients. One of these was: 'I wish that I had let myself be happier'.

If you Google 'how to be happy' there are 5,970 million results! One of the results proclaims - 'You Deserve to Be Happy'. Every bookshop has a section filled with 'self-help' titles, and there is an industry of happiness gurus and motivational speakers providing advice on the topic. Of course, if you live in the poorest half of the planet this might be viewed as a 'First World problem'; the fundamental question here is more likely to be 'How do I survive?'

Yet in the Sermon on the Mount (often called the Beatitudes) Jesus clearly spells things out for us:

> 'How happy are the poor in spirit;
> theirs is the kingdom of heaven.
> Happy the gentle:
> They shall have the earth for their heritage.
> Happy those who mourn for they shall be comforted.
> Happy those who hunger and thirst for what is right:
> they shall be satisfied.
> Happy the merciful:
> they shall have mercy shown them.

Happy the pure in heart:
they shall see God.
Happy the peacemakers:
for they shall be called sons of God.
Happy those who are persecuted in the cause of right:
theirs is the kingdom of heaven.'
(MATTHEW 5:2-10)

Happiness involves being gentle and merciful, striving for justice and becoming peacemakers. All of these beatitudes involve other people - you can rarely attain happiness on your own, there is no such thing as 'private happiness'. The philosopher John-Paul Sartre famously wrote: 'Hell is other people'. For Jesus, the *kingdom of heaven* is other people. In the upside-down world of the Gospel we can only be happy if others are happy, we can only have mercy shown to us, if we show mercy to others. We can only be 'saved' by saving others. There can be no justice and peace until everyone has justice and peace. Our happiness is tied inextricably to the happiness and well-being of others - in the words of John Donne, 'No man is an island'. There is nothing more joyful than giving joy to others and ensuring the world is a better place for our presence. The message of Western consumerism is 'Me, myself and I', whereas Jesus tells us that true happiness starts and ends with the happiness of others.

For Bonnie Ware's patients their final regret was that they couldn't turn things around. We however, still have some time left if we wish to try living out the Beatitudes.

83

—

Service

'You call me Master and Lord, and rightly; so I am. If I, then, the Lord and Master, have washed your feet, you should wash each other's feet. I have given you an example so that you may copy what I have done to you.'
(JOHN 13:13-15)

During the covid-19 pandemic there were countless examples of extraordinary acts of service from doctors and nurses and other healthcare workers; continually going above and beyond what was expected of them in the service of their patients. As the health service reached breaking point, patients and families reported on the extraordinary care taken by thousands of ordinary people, exhausting themselves on a daily basis with thousands of small acts of self-sacrifice, kindness and care for others.

When Jesus meets with his disciples at the Last Supper he washes their feet. Jesus knows that he will soon no longer be with them, and there is a touching intimacy and vulnerability about this action, something that would normally have been done by a lowly servant. As usual, Jesus turns the existing hierarchy and established order on its head - true authority comes not from position in society but from loving service.

Jesus then tells them to do the same to each other - his message is that yes, he is lord and master, but also a humble servant.

DOING CHRISTIANITY

He is commissioning his disciples for a life of service - he holds before them an example to follow. He even washes the feet of Judas, knowing that he will later betray him - no-one, not even our enemies, is exempt from the love of Jesus, and no-one should be excluded from our loving service either. There are no feet that cannot be washed. When we become 'washers of feet' we move from theory to practice, we don't just study and admire the teaching of Jesus, we become participants in his work.

Peter tells Jesus, 'You shall never wash my feet'; he sees it as demeaning for Jesus, and like many of us, when confronted with something which we find uncomfortable, he resists. He wants to cling to the established order, the way things have always been done. But Jesus insists, saying it is essential. We too need to humbly accept loving service when it is offered and recognise the presence of Christ in those who care for us.

Jesus ends by saying 'Now that you know this, happiness will be yours if you behave accordingly'. It is a simple rule for life - if you want to be happy yourself, then serve others.

During the Last Supper Jesus gives the disciples his body and blood, the sacrament of the Eucharist. However, our world is full of sacramental moments; each act of service is a kind of holy sacrament, a grace-filled moment. There is no distinction between the sacred and the secular – God is to be found in ordinary events and activities, all the messy nooks and crannies of our lives.

During the pandemic there were all sorts of 'feet being washed' in our hospitals - the feet of 'saints and sinners' alike. Whether they were aware of it or not, those doctors and nurses were ministers of holy sacraments, putting into practice Jesus' call to selflessly serve one another in our hour of need.

Whose feet am I being called to wash?

84

—

Thy Kingdom Come

'Thy kingdom come, thy will be done, on earth
as it is in heaven.'
(MATTHEW 6:10)

We are all connected to each other. We sometimes imagine that we are alone or separate, and this can be a kind of prison for us. We can become selfish, seeing ourselves as the centre of the universe. And the more we focus on ourselves, the less happy we become. When we do think of, or love others, it is often reserved for our nearest and dearest only. We forget that we are part of a whole, we are links in a chain, connected through God to all our brothers and sisters throughout the world, indeed to all of nature - to all the Universe. This is what we mean when we say in the 'Our Father' - 'thy kingdom come'. This is God's kingdom, we are all part of it, and we have an important role to play in its ongoing daily re-creation.

When we see the world this way, we understand the importance of widening our circles of love to include everyone and everything. We see ourselves not as individual souls struggling through life but part of a greater whole, key co-workers in a bigger plan for humanity. Without our contribution, our compassion and care, the universe is slightly less whole and more fragmented. We are called to be an active participant (not an observer) in God's ongoing transformation of our world. As John Henry Newman put it, 'I am a link in a chain, a bond of connection between persons. He has not created me for naught. I shall do good; I shall do His work'. We have been created for a reason; we have our part to play (some work which no one else can do). If we are in a prison of our own separateness and aloneness then the key to freedom is in our own hands. Many preachers have told us 'you will get your reward in heaven', but Jesus says, 'you will get your reward now, the kingdom of heaven is at hand'.

When the Pharisees question Jesus about the kingdom, he tells them, 'you must know, the kingdom of God is among you.' Christ the King is not in the 'highest heavens', he is among us, waiting for us to play our part, not just in *praying* 'thy kingdom come', but helping to make it happen.

What is my role in making 'thy kingdom come'?

85

—

Liberation

When Christ freed us, he meant us to remain free.
(GALATIANS 5:1)

In the 1960s a way of thinking about religion developed in Latin America called liberation theology. According to liberation theologians, much traditional theology is concerned with dogma and abstract religious concepts, often failing to come up with an understanding of God that has consequences in real life. Theology, if it is to have any relevance, must be rooted in the practical realities of everyday life. It must address the key structural issues of poverty, economic injustice and inequality. A theology that is not grounded in these everyday realities can end up being 'art for art's sake'. Unless we understand the need for 'an option for the poor' (solidarity with the poor) then we can end up ignoring the injustice and suffering endured by half the world.

Christ does not just point out that there is hunger in the world, he tells us that the hungry are our brothers and sisters, and that we are standing by while they starve. God has created the world and everything in it for all of us to share. St John Chrysostom offers those of us who live in the developed world a challenging assessment of this gospel: 'The rich are in possession of the goods of the poor, even if they have acquired them honestly or inherited them legally.' He goes on to say, 'Not to share our own wealth with the poor is theft from the poor and deprivation of their means of life; we do not possess our own wealth, but theirs.'

Archbishop Oscar Romero of El Salvador said: 'The ones who have a voice must speak for those who are voiceless'. The gospel message preached by Jesus is not always a comfortable one. As Archbishop Romero pointed out: 'a gospel that doesn't unsettle, a word of God that doesn't get under anyone's skin, a word of God that doesn't touch the real sin of the society in which it is proclaimed - what gospel is that?'

On day one of Jesus' ministry he goes to the synagogue and reads from Isaiah: 'He has sent me to bring the good news to the poor, to proclaim liberty to captives ... to set the downtrodden free'. His message is a spiritual one, but he recognises that it is difficult for a person to hear the word of God if they are hungry. He feeds the five thousand because he knows that although 'man cannot live on bread alone', he cannot live at all without food. For centuries the churches focussed their attention on individual or personal sin, but Pope John Paul II often highlighted 'institutional evil' and 'structural sin'.

Often this powerful message gets lost, because it is uncomfortable and challenging for those of us living in relative affluence in the developed world. But Pope Francis says: 'I prefer a church which is bruised, hurting and dirty because it has been out on the streets, rather than a church which is unhealthy from being confined and from clinging to its own security'. For those with the courage to preach social justice in oppressed nations such theology is viewed as subversion, a dangerous threat to existing power structures. It is worth remembering that if Jesus had just been a teacher and healer he might not have been executed. He was killed primarily because his call for God's justice unsettled the political authorities of the day.

Archbishop Romero also gave his life for preaching the gospel, assassinated in 1980 by gunmen, whilst saying mass in a hospice for cancer patients.

....

Can I make an 'option for the poor'?

86

—

Love one another

'I give you a new commandment: love one another;
just as I have loved you, you also must love one
another. By this love you have for one another,
everyone will know that you are my disciples.'
(JOHN 13:34-35)

We all sometimes struggle with the 'Big Questions' of life. Why are we here? Does life have a purpose? What does it all mean?

Jesus tells us that the answer to such questions is a simple one. He reminds us that religion is about what we do, and specifically how we love. In the extract above from the Last Supper, Jesus is aware that his time on earth is coming to an end, and he is clear and direct with his disciples - 'Love one another'. Here is the answer to all our questions in just three words. He then follows this up with the crucial and life changing - 'As I have loved you.' Jesus is saying that if we can understand how much we are loved by God, then we can discover the freedom and confidence to pass this love on to others, and not just our family and friends, but our 'enemies' too. We can see our neighbour in a new way, not as someone separate from us, an opponent perhaps, but as a brother or sister.

This transformative power of love changes lives. Remember, we are not beloved by God because of our 'goodness' - we are loved by God because God is good. And this love sets us free to love others, and the more love we receive, the more love we can give away. This revelation was to transform the lives of the disciples.

If we are not careful we can mistake love for an emotion, that 'fuzzy feeling' of being 'in love' perhaps. But love is mostly a choice, a commitment - we choose to love, and by so doing we bring meaning to our lives and the world. Like everything else in life, love doesn't just happen - we have to work at it, we have to will it into existence! If you struggle with this then start small - love those closest to you. If you can do this, then there is no reason why you can't extend that love outwards like the ripples on a pond. Before you know it your circle of love will expand until you are loving everybody, including perhaps, 'those who persecute you' (Matthew 5:44-45).

When we love we connect with God, whether we know it or not, whether we believe in God or not. The choice to love is the most important thing (not what we believe in our heads). Hence many loving atheists are practical Christians, and some who profess belief in their heads and on their lips, are 'practicing atheists' or 'Christians in Name Only'. As John says, 'Anyone who fails to love can never have known God, because God is love' (1 John 4:8).

You might be reading this and finding it difficult to believe in God, and that's OK. If the disciples who lived with Jesus had their doubts, and they did, then we too must expect our periods of uncertainty. But whatever you feel about God's existence, every human being I have ever met believes in Love. And as Metropolitan Anthony Bloom said, "What is the basic difference between saying 'I know that love exists' and saying 'I know that God exists'?"

God is Love; and in the end, Love is all that really matters.

....

Have you ever stopped to recognise and
appreciate the love God has for you? Stop
reading now for a moment. Sitting quietly in your
chair just pause and appreciate God loving you,
as you gently breathe in and out. From before
your first infant breath, to beyond your last, you
are loved. You have always been loved dearly
by God, and this love will never end. The entire
universe (including you) was created by Love
and is sustained by it. For those with eyes to see
and open hearts, it is everywhere, waiting to be
breathed in, and breathed out (passed on to
others). Take as long as you like to rest quietly in
this love for a while.

87

—

Jesus is Alive!

The angel spoke; and he said to the women, 'There is no need for you to be afraid. I know you are looking for Jesus, who was crucified. He is not here, for he has risen, as he said he would. Come and see the place where he lay, then go quickly and tell his disciples, "He has risen from the dead" ...'
(MATTHEW 28:5-7)

Everything changed when Christ rose from the dead on the third day - nothing would ever be the same again. Without the Resurrection the Jesus story would have been an interesting footnote in history - a miracle worker, a holy man, remembered with fondness by his friends. As each of the apostles passed away, the memories would have dimmed, and the Jesus movement would probably have withered away, a few stories passed on to grandchildren perhaps and then nothing left but folklore, and then nothing.

The resurrection means that we are able to say, 'Jesus is alive!' in the present tense. He has conquered death, not just for himself, but for all peoples and all times. It enables us to say, 'He lives among us', not a figure from history, but a living presence - in the present. The Risen Christ transcends time and space - he is available everywhere to everybody.

For the disciples the resurrection meant that Jesus had fulfilled the promise he had made to them. He was truly the Son of God. He appeared to them in various places in the days that followed, enabling Thomas the 'doubting disciple' to place his hands in his wounds and proclaim, 'My Lord and my God'. More than just an ordinary man, the Word made flesh, the Risen Lord, ready to fill his followers with his Holy Spirit so that the Christian Church could begin, and then spread to every corner of the globe.

The cross and resurrection of Jesus are not historical events to be pondered from afar - they reflect our own lived experience, our own falling and rising. Here we find hope, that the personal darkness we often experience will eventually be followed by the morning light. Here is proof that God's grace can lift us out of every situation, no matter how desperate and hopeless it might appear. Hence the phrase 'We are an Easter people'; in spite of all our failings and flaws we live with the hope of something better, we know that good will always triumph over evil.

For many Christians the resurrection is significant because it signals that there is life for us too, after our own physical death. But this is to only grasp the half of it. The resurrection is something for us to experience in every moment whilst we still live! We share in the resurrection whenever we share the love and joy of God with each other; if you look carefully you will see the Risen Christ in all you meet. Jesus is raised from the dead whenever we choose to transform our lives, and the lives of others, by acts of kindness. We bring Jesus to life by our daily attempts to faithfully live out the gospel, by what we do, and how we treat one another.

Can I see and encounter the Risen Christ today?

88

—

Preach the Gospel

'Go, therefore, make disciples of all the nations; baptise them in the name of the Father and of the Son and of the Holy Spirit, and teach them to observe the commands I gave you. And know that I am with you always; yes, to the end of time.'
(MATTHEW 28:19-20)

If you are reading this and you are Christian, then you are a Christian because someone passed the faith on to you. After Pentecost, the disciples, inspired with courage by the Spirit, began their work of conversion. Christianity spread from one to another, passing down through the generations. Perhaps it has come to you through your parents and grandparents, or perhaps someone from outside your family, or some writer of a book; someone told you about Jesus, and you began to believe. The faith has been passed to you - a person-to-person transmission, from Jesus himself, over two millennia.

Jesus didn't intend to start a small insular sect; he wanted a worldwide movement, hence the instruction 'to make disciples of all nations.' It is a task we all share. Like a rugby player who is in possession of the ball, our job is to make sure 'the play' continues by passing it on to someone else. The message of Jesus has to be given away.

How do we do this? Probably not through hours of instruction and learning. Follow the example of Saint Francis of Assisi who is reported to have said, 'Preach the gospel at all times. If necessary, use words.' Another version of his teaching is, 'It is no use walking anywhere to preach unless our walking is our preaching.' It has often been said that our lives are the only Bible many people will read. Cardinal Newman's prayer sums this up beautifully: 'let me preach you without preaching; teach you without teaching; not by words but by example, by the catching influence of who I am and what I do.' We are called to be Christ for others.

Such a task is daunting, but those original eleven, ill-educated, impoverished disciples managed to succeed. This of course is only possible because they and we, do not work alone. Matthew ends his entire gospel with Jesus' words, 'And know that I am with you always; yes to the end time.'

....

Can I 'preach without preaching'?

89

—

Continuing his work

*'I tell you most solemnly, whoever believes
in me will perform the same works as I do
myself, he will perform even greater works,
because I am going to the Father.'*
(JOHN 14:12)

In the 1990s the phrase 'What would Jesus do?' became popular in the United States and elsewhere (wristbands and bracelets were produced with the initials WWJD). The phrase became a personal motto to remind people to act in a manner that would reflect the way Jesus might respond in any given situation. However, 'What would Jesus do?' can perhaps appear as an abstract idea - 'what would Jesus do *if he were here now*?' But Christ *is here now*, he is alive through us and in us. God's plans are being worked out through us, every day, in each present moment. 'What would Jesus do? could be replaced by 'What is Christ doing through me now?'

In this extract from the Last Supper Jesus is saying in effect, my power is now yours - through the Spirit, you now have the grace to love, to bless, to comfort and to heal. You are the way in which the incarnation continues.

This incarnation is not just an event in Galilee two thousand years ago; it pervades and suffuses every aspect of our lives today. All love is Christ incarnate. When we love another, Christ is loving that person. When we forgive someone, Christ is forgiving them too. When we generously give our time to a friend, Christ is blessing them through us. When we share in the pain and suffering of another, Christ is there too sharing our burdens. The incarnate Christ patiently awaits the hand of compassion we offer to each other. Christ not only lives in us, but anoints us to continue his saving work with everyone we encounter.

Therefore, to sin is to ignore our calling to be Christ to all - to refuse to take responsibility for caring for and loving ourself, our neighbour and our planet. It is deliberately deciding that we don't need others, and they don't need us.

Christ has saved us not as individuals, but as a community, as a people - we are all bound together in this enterprise. There is no distinction or barrier between us and God, and between us and everyone else. We are all one in Christ, who becomes incarnate as *Emmanuel*, which means 'God is with us'.

Later in the Supper, John tells us that Jesus says, *'Father, may they be one in us, as you are in me and I am in you, so that the world may believe it was you who sent me'* (John 17:21).

Am I ready to continue the work of Christ?

STEP SEVEN

A New Way of Praying

If you are like me, you will have frequent periods when prayer is dry and difficult, or in some cases nonsensical. We can get the feeling that God is distant or separated from us. At times like these I often like to picture myself swimming in the sea on a warm, sunny day. There is something very liberating and relaxing when you drift along, feeling part of the vast ocean, just bobbing around, at one with the water and with nature. This is a good way to envisage God, not someone separate, but like the ocean, someone in whom we 'live and move and have our being' - all around us, supporting us, connected to us. Like the air we breathe. We are part of God, and God is part of us.

The author of 'The Cloud of Unknowing' writes that asking, 'Who is God?' is ultimately the wrong question, 'because it means you are still in your head. Get out of your head and into your heart.' His central message is that God is not an idea to be grasped but a loving presence to be enjoyed.

A Christianity that doesn't enable people to have an authentic prayer life isn't really preaching the good news. Step

7 is an attempt to reinvigorate our prayer lives by expanding what we mean by prayer and how we 'do it'. There is no magic formula for prayer and anyone can do it, anytime, anywhere. We don't need to go to a special building and there are no essential words or phrases. In this section we examine meditative prayer, listening, silence and prayer as action. Ultimately prayer isn't something we believe in, it's something we do, like breathing or swimming. In the end our goal is for all of life to become a prayer.

90

—

Lived prayer

'if you are bringing your offering to the altar and there remember that your brother has something against you, leave your offering there before the altar, go and be reconciled with your brother first, and then come back and present your offering.'
(MATTHEW: 5:23-25)

For many of us prayer is difficult, for some it appears to be meaningless or pointless. We can end up simply reciting words without thought or without being fully present. At other times our prayers can resemble a shopping list of items which we present to God for his deliberation. This kind of prayer is often very ego-centric - what can I get God to do for me.

But prayer is not about 'changing God's mind' or bending him to our will. It is about opening up to the power of the Holy Spirit to come and change us, and then through us, to touch the lives of others.

In Thessalonians, St Paul says we are to 'pray constantly'. What on earth could this mean? He certainly doesn't expect us to be on our knees 24/7, for most of us that would be neither practical nor desirable.

The essence of the Gospel is that all our life should be a prayer (not just the five minutes before we climb into bed). Prayer isn't just thinking things or saying words – it is a way of living in the presence of God.

We cannot separate prayer from action. Some people say 'God never answers my prayers or solves my problems', but God expects us to be part of the solution. We must expect to participate through our actions in the work that God does for the people we pray for. Spending an hour with a lonely neighbour is a prayer; volunteering in a local charity shop is a prayer; calling a friend who has health problems and listening to their worries is a prayer; reading your children a bedtime story is a prayer; phoning your elderly parent or grandparent and listening to them talk about their day is a prayer. In the words of Metropolitan Anthony Bloom, 'A prayer makes sense only if it is lived'.

Jesus highlights the importance of actions by saying that it is hard to pray if you have some unresolved issues or conflict in your life. Reconcile with your brother first, and then come back to the altar. He condemns the scribes who make 'a show of lengthy prayers' while 'swallowing the property of widows'. Prayer is communication with God which is of course a two-way thing. If we are to be at one with God, and if we acknowledge his presence in us, then there can be no distinction between our prayer time and our daily life. Worship is not an end in itself - it is about being transformed, so that all of life becomes a prayer. This is what Jesus meant when he asked us to 'worship in spirit and in truth'.

....

How can I develop the mindset so that all of life becomes a prayer?

91

—

Lettuce pray

*'the judgements you give are the judgements
you will get, and the amount you measure out
is the amount you will be given.'*
(MATTHEW 7:1-3)

The Zen Buddhist monk Thich Nhat Hanh describes the problems of growing lettuce in his book 'Peace is Every Step'. He says that if you are growing a lettuce and it doesn't grow so well, *you don't blame the lettuce*. A good gardener will try to find out why it isn't growing so well - you might need to water it more, move it into a sunnier position, give it some fertilizer or get rid of the greenfly. At any rate you never blame the lettuce - it's doing its best in the conditions it's in.

However, if we have difficulties with family, friends or loved ones we almost always blame the other person. They are at fault. Such fault-finding and blaming doesn't achieve what we want it to achieve, and pointing out how they are failing step-by-step using logical reasoning is rarely successful. Like the lettuce we have to take time to understand what it is they need if they are to grow. The only way to produce change is to understand, and show that you understand. If people are to grow they need care, compassion and above all, love. Love is the fertiliser - unconditional love can make the human heart grow in the most difficult of circumstances. It produces rich soil that nourishes us, and helps us to flourish when we are battered by the storms of life. It is an almost universal rule that we can't change another person by criticizing them or pointing out their faults.

However, when we love and understand, then we often produce the conditions for the miracle of change in the other person to take place. It is difficult of course, to love another, if that person is hurting you. This is happening because the other person is suffering, and this suffering is spilling out and affecting you. It is a cry for help and understanding, not an opportunity for spite or criticism. Once we can see that, then we can also begin to understand the need to examine that plank in our own eye, before we lovingly help our brother or sister take the splinter out of their eye.

As Anthony Bloom said, 'Unless we look at a person and see the beauty there is in this person, we can contribute nothing to him... Christ looked at everyone he met, at the prostitute, at the thief, and saw the beauty hidden there. Perhaps it was distorted, perhaps damaged, but it was beauty none the less, and what he did was to call out this beauty.'

....

Before I approach God in prayer, who in my life, do I need to understand and love?

92

—

Be still

'It is Mary who has chosen the better part.'
(LUKE 10:42)

Blaise Pascal was a 17th century French mathematician, physicist, inventor and Catholic theologian who once said: 'All of humanity's problems stem from man's inability to sit quietly in a room alone.'

In the view of the Jesuit theologian Karl Rahner, Christianity in the West needs to rediscover its mystical roots if it is survive into the future. His point was that people need to have some kind of *inner religious experience* if they are to really live life as a follower of Christ. Putting the gospel into practice or making sense of religious doctrines is difficult unless we have some personal experience of God. The word 'mystical' here means the movement away from mere belief systems to personal experience of the divine.

Luke describes how Jesus visits the house of the sisters, Martha and Mary. Whilst Martha busies herself with getting dinner ready, Mary sits at the feet of Jesus and listens to him. Martha is cross, and asks Jesus to tell Mary to help her. Jesus replies 'Martha, Martha, you worry and fret about so many things, and yet few are needed, indeed only one. It is Mary who has chosen the better part ...'

There is a lot to take from this passage. Martha is clearly an amazing person, inviting Jesus and his companions in, and then selflessly preparing food for them all. Discontent only begins to appear when she compares herself to her 'lazy' sister who is just sitting there. Comparison is a killer - call to mind those occasions when you have compared yourself to others, and found your life wanting. Comparing your life to others never changes anything or anyone; it just steals your joy.

Jesus' response to Martha is loving. He shows her the path she needs to take to find peace - stop worrying about so much, there is only one thing that matters - relationship. It has also been suggested that perhaps Martha was obsessed with providing Jesus with an elaborate banquet when a small, simple meal was all that was needed?

Mary has understood that being with Jesus, and listening to him, is the only thing that matters in this moment. Many have seen this as an invitation to practice meditation or contemplation, to 'Be still and know that I am God' (Psalm 46:10). In this form of prayer God is not demanding anything of us, we aren't supposed to be earning a gold medal in meditation or becoming the perfect exponent of contemplation. Like Mary we are just meant to be there. That's all.

Most of us weren't taught about contemplative prayer as children - our prayers usually consist of words: thoughts, worship and requests expressed in language. Interestingly, 99% of young people don't go to church or participate in traditional liturgical worship but are nevertheless quite keen on meditation and stillness. Perhaps they are on to something. Thankfully this type of prayer is now taught in many Catholic primary and secondary schools in Britain and Ireland.

Contemplative prayer based on silence and quiet has existed throughout Christian history. Through quiet contemplation we open our whole being to God, going beyond words and feelings. Simply being present in the moment is sufficient.

Contemplative prayer is often called 'resting in God'. It is acknowledging that God lives in us, sustaining and loving us in each breath we take. It is realising that we and everyone and everything is the way that God is present in the world.

Jesus certainly would have prayed with his disciples in the synagogue, but the gospels also tell us that he continually seeks out solitude and silence. He spends forty days in the desert before he begins his public ministry, and Luke records that 'he would always go off to some place where he could be alone and pray' (Luke 5:16). 'When you pray' he tells his disciples, 'go to your private room and, when you have shut your door, pray to your Father who is in that secret place...' (Matthew 6:6).

Can you just sit still for five minutes each day? Incorporating a period of daily stillness can be a wonderful antidote to the worry and stress of daily life. Such prayer is wordless, but some people find it helpful to gently focus on a phrase from scripture, or a simple prayer such as 'Come Lord Jesus' or the 'Jesus Prayer': *Lord Jesus Christ, Son of the Living God, have mercy on me, a sinner* (this prayer can be easily linked to your breathing). There is no right or wrong way to do this. Thoughts and distractions will inevitably come and go, but just return gently to your word or phrase, and stay calm and relaxed. After a while silence will come, and you can enjoy resting here for as long as you wish. St John Vianney once found an old man in the church just staring at the tabernacle. John asked him what he was doing and the man explained, 'I look at him and he looks at me'.

At other times you might imagine yourself, like Mary, sitting wordlessly at the feet of Jesus, or on a mountain top or lakeside. Close your eyes and practice breathing slowly and deeply, breathing out the stress and tension in your body, and breathing in God's Spirit of peace and calm. When your mind wanders just gently draw your attention back to your breathing. By stilling our racing thoughts, and making a space of calm, we can better recognize the presence of God within us.

Sometimes this type of prayer will be difficult and boring, but at other times you may feel a tremendous sense of peace. Try and commit to this on a daily basis. It's fine to start small, five minutes a day at first, but then you might want to increase your contemplative periods to 15 minutes or more. After a while, you will look forward to these periods of quiet calm and be disappointed if you miss them. And don't give up - even if you find it difficult and are constantly distracted; many of us just can't cope with silence, but if you persist you will get there. Remember that prayer is not an exam in which you are trying to get an A grade. Don't look for 'success' in your prayer life - being there, being present is all that matters. Intention and commitment are everything.

Of course, this connection with the divine may also spill over into other areas of your life and you might find yourself walking in the park contemplatively or sitting on the bus contemplatively. It will almost certainly lead us to think in a calmer, more compassionate way, less concerned with our own ego, and less judgemental of everyone and everything. Other prayers may well flow from our contemplation such as thanksgiving, joy and adoration. When we become aware of God's presence it enables us to enjoy the moment more, and the more practice you get at being present, the more God's presence can be appreciated.

In the morning, long before dawn, he got up and left the house, and went off to a lonely place and prayed there. (Mark 1:35-36).

Try starting with five minutes a day sitting at the feet of Jesus, and you too will have chosen the better part.

93

—

Awe

*Jesus cured the paralysed man and those who
saw it 'were all astounded and praised God,
and were filled with awe ...'*
(LUKE 5:26)

'That's awesome' is an over-used phrase today - something people might say when they've just watched a great YouTube clip. However, sometimes when we climb to the top of a mountain, stand at the water's edge on the seashore, walk through a forest, or sit quietly by a lake and watch the sunset, we experience real awe.

Awe is wonder and reverence when confronted by the beauty of God's creation. We can also experience it sitting in our garden, looking at a tree, listening to a bird sing, or gazing at a flower on a windowsill. Such events remind us that God is here, that God is in this scene, that God is with us. By paying attention to the natural world our mood lightens and we allow ourselves to be moved by the Spirit. Pope Francis puts it like this: 'God has written a precious book, *whose letters are the multitude of created things present in the universe*' (*Laudato Si*).

Our own world sometimes seems so small. At times we need to look at the night sky and stand in wonder at the vastness of the universe and the untold number of stars and galaxies (the edge of the observable universe is 46 billion light years away). Sensing and enjoying God's presence in all these moments is a gift from God to you. Take a deep breath and recognise with St Paul that there is 'One God who is Father of all, over all, through all and within all' (Ephesians 4:6).

The Jesuit theologian Walter Burghardt described contemplation as taking a 'long, loving look at the Real'. We gaze at the reality, the one-ness of the created world and the Creator, and we see God taking a long, loving look back at us.

If we want to know who God is then we need to acknowledge and marvel at the beauty and goodness of something outside of ourselves. We must then understand that everything in the universe, all of God's creation including ourselves is beautiful and good. At that moment we see God - and we see Him looking back at us. We are one with God and the whole of creation.

The natural world fills us with awe because we can see, behind it all, the hand of a loving God. At the very start of John's Gospel, we read about God's creative power: 'Through him all things came to be, not one thing had its being but through him. All that came to be had life in him and that light was the light of men, a light that shines in the dark...' (John 1:2-5)

....

When a person receives the sacrament of Confirmation the bishop extends his hands over the candidates and asks God to 'fill them with the Spirit of wonder and awe in your presence.' Take time to stand in awe today and see, in the natural world, the Creator God extending his hand over you.

94

—

The Pharisee and the tax collector

'The tax collector stood some distance away, not daring to raise his eyes to heaven; but he beat his breast and said, "God, be merciful to me, a sinner". This man I tell you, went home again at rights with God...'
(LUKE 18:13-14)

If you've ever felt ever so slightly pleased with yourself for your religious faith then this parable of the Pharisee and the tax collector is for you. When these two go up to the Temple to pray the Pharisee says: 'I thank you, God, that I am not grasping, unjust, adulterous like the rest of mankind, and particularly that I am not like this tax collector here'. Note that the Pharisee is a very religious person. He fasts twice a week (more often than the law requires) and he pays a tithe (a tenth of all he gets). Outwardly he conforms to every religious requirement, and is no doubt admired and respected by his peers, perhaps held up as an example to others.

However, Jesus tells us that he prays 'to himself' not to God! Imprisoned by his own ego and sense of superiority, he is incapable of an authentic connection with anything beyond himself. If he is to know the God who is loving mercy, then he must recognise his need of that mercy, his need of forgiveness. But he doesn't think he needs God. When he leaves the Temple he is exactly the same person as when he arrived.

The tax collector on the other hand, clearly knows he is a sinner. He stands apart in humility, not daring to 'raise his eyes to heaven'; the only person he judges is himself. In spite of his sin he has the self-awareness and honesty to beg God for forgiveness and mercy. He knows he needs it. He leaves the Temple forgiven by God.

The outwardly good man is not really good at all - Jesus tells us that whilst the apparent sinner goes home again 'at rights with God; the other did not'. This echoes Jesus' scathing denunciation of the Pharisees in Matthew 23:25: 'You who clean the outside of cup and dish and leave the inside full of extortion and intemperance.'

The Pharisee is so proud and self assured in his own religiosity that he asks God for nothing, and in return, receives nothing. The tax collector asks for everything, and in return he receives everything - the forgiveness of God. The man who humbled himself has been 'exalted'.

He has also given us a perfect prayer: 'God, be merciful to me, a sinner.'

....

Am I more like the Pharisee or the tax collector?
Spend some time today with the tax collector,
praying his prayer and humbly throwing yourself
on the mercy of God.

95

—

Gratitude

'Were not all ten made clean? The other nine
where are they?'
(LUKE 17:18)

L uke records how Jesus cured ten lepers, but only one,
a Samaritan came back to thank him. Gratitude is an
important human quality; by showing thankfulness we
acknowledge that there is goodness in our life, and that we are
blessed. By expressing gratitude we recognise that the source
of that goodness comes from outside of ourselves, either from
God or from somebody else. Gratitude connects us to a world
outside of ourselves, to something bigger than ourselves.

We might feel gratitude for past blessings such as a loving upbringing, continued good health or well-being, or the
friendship and kindness of others. Research has shown that
a feeling of gratitude for the gift of life leads to hope for the
future and a more optimistic mindset.

Gratitude is something that can be cultivated but for many
of us it does not come easily. Some of us may feel beset with
difficulties, thinking there is little in life to be grateful for. For
those with a 'glass half empty' mindset it can be difficult to
cultivate an attitude of thankfulness. Often it is a matter of
perspective; we fail to count the blessings we have because

we can't see them. If we consider the gift of life we have been given, if we can understand that the God who created the entire universe chose to create us, because the world needed one of us, unique and beautiful, if we can begin to feel the love and care that God showers upon us (if only we could see it), then an attitude of humble gratefulness can begin to take root in our soul. This love that God has for us is of course often expressed through the love and attention shown us by others.

Gratitude helps us to focus on what we have, rather than what we lack. In the West we expect so much, and we get cross if we don't get what we think we are entitled to. This sense of entitlement saps the spirit. However, when we see everything as a gift then we stop thinking about what we 'deserve' and start saying 'thank you' for what we have. And thankfulness multiplies - the more grateful a person becomes the more things they seem to be grateful for. Conversely, if you focus on what you haven't got you will never have enough.

Perhaps the greatest prayer you can say is 'Thank You'. If you find prayer difficult then concentrate on gratitude - thank God for your life and the opportunities you have been given - look closely and you will find more things than you realise to be grateful for.

Nine lepers that Jesus healed did not show gratitude, only one came back to thank him. When it comes to us, do we take our life for granted, or do we take it with gratitude?

....

Find opportunities to show gratitude today.

DOING CHRISTIANITY

96

—

Listening

'Speak, Lord, your servant is listening.'
(1 Samuel 3:10)

One of my friends is renowned as a great conversationalist. People love to have a chat with him and seek him out. I discovered his secret early on - he doesn't say very much - but he's a fantastic listener. You may have noticed that in many conversations people aren't really that interested in what you have to say, but are very interested in telling you all about themselves. In the words of a T-shirt I once saw, 'I hear you but I'm not listening!' Not listening diminishes the other person, whereas listening attentively invites them to matter and thrive.

Psychologists and counsellors have observed that men are often much worse than women at listening. Studies have shown that when women pour out their fears and difficulties to their partners, many men will immediately suggest solutions. They think they are being 'helpful' - psychological studies have shown that most men enjoy solving problems, but this just irritates their partner. Most of us aren't necessarily looking for solutions (sometimes the problem can't be solved anyway), we just want someone to listen.

Dietrich Bonhoeffer said: 'He who can no longer listen to

his brother will soon be no longer listening to God either.' How do you view your conversations with God? Are you doing all the talking? Is prayer a monologue, presenting lists and petitions? It's good to tell God our fears and worries, in fact Jesus tells us to do this, and promises that he will 'give us rest'. But do we ever listen? God is always trying to teach us, trying to love us, trying to reveal himself to us, but more often than not we don't make time to listen. Although listening generally needs silence we can, with practice, do it anywhere, even in the busiest environments, if we can quieten our thoughts and open our hearts. Many find it easier to listen when connected to nature - just sitting under a tree or walking in some green space.

What if you are not sure if anyone is listening to you? Well, many psychologists have pointed out the benefits of talking to yourself (most of us do it anyway without thinking). We constantly talk to ourselves about our lives, our problems, our hopes and dreams. This is prayer too, because God is listening. This realisation can help us to see that God is ever present, always involved in our 'self-talk', always part of our conversation.

God is unlikely to address us in a loud booming voice, but he is constantly communicating with us. He wants to tell us things, to draw alongside us, to offer us comfort and give us energy. Make space for him, find silence, and be attentive to his voice.

....

Take a moment to heed the advice of the Psalmist (95:7): 'If only you would listen to him today'.

97

—

Our Father

'In your prayers do not babble as the pagans do, for they think that by using many words they will make themselves heard. Do not be like them; your Father knows what you need before you ask him. So you should pray like this...'
(MATTHEW 6:7-9)

Jesus teaches his disciples the Lord's Prayer: 'Our Father, Who art in Heaven, hallowed be Thy name; Thy Kingdom come, Thy will be done on earth as it is in Heaven. Give us this day our daily bread; and forgive us our trespasses as we forgive those who trespass against us; and lead us not into temptation, but deliver us from evil.'

Did you skim read this prayer? We say the Lord's Prayer so often that if we are not careful it all just drifts past us or we end up babbling like 'the pagans do!' It is worth stopping to ponder this prayer that Jesus taught us, as it encapsulates the Gospel message in just a few simple lines. As a wise teacher once advised when asked how to pray, 'say the Our Father, and take an hour to say it'.

If we are not careful the focus of our prayer can begin with *me*, 'what do I want', 'what do I need.' The focus here is not on me but on our joint endeavour - it is on *Our* Father (not My Father). As members of God's family we can join Jesus in calling God our heavenly Father. The word Jesus uses is 'Abba' - best translated as 'Dad' in modern English. This form of address would have been a shock to Jesus' listeners, who would have been used to prayers which extolled the majesty and otherness of God, not his closeness and intimacy. 'Father' speaks of a new, less distant, more loving relationship between us and God.

We then pray for the coming of God's kingdom - this is a kingdom not of armies, thrones and worldly power but a kingdom of justice and peace. We of course are co-creators of this Kingdom and that is to be our principal task in life. Earth is not a preparation for a heaven that is to come, it is the place where heaven is brought into being by our actions and our life with Christ - the Kingdom of Heaven is at hand.

We ask for our 'daily bread', the practical and spiritual nourishment to sustain us, and we ask this not just for ourselves, but for all in the world who go hungry. We then pray for forgiveness from God in the same way that we forgive those who hurt us. The Gospel makes clear that you cannot live an authentic life unless you are prepared to forgive. Forgiveness is the essential foundation of all our relationships, and it is because God has first forgiven us that we are enabled to forgive others.

Jesus then asks us to pray, 'lead us not into temptation but deliver us from evil.' Life was hard in Jesus' time, and he often tells his disciples that they will face times of crisis or difficulty, testing times. The prayer is saying, don't give us our cross or our trial, until you've prepared us for it, until you've given us all we need to be able to get through it. Deliverance from evil means being released from the self-centeredness and sinfulness which prevent us from living an authentic life.

Take time now to pray the 'Our Father' slowly, as if for the first time, savouring each phrase and what it means for you. Notice how the prayer begins with God and ends with you.

98

Justice and the persistent widow

'will not God see justice done to his chosen who cry to him day and night...'
(LUKE 18:7)

Jesus tells a parable about a widow and a judge. The widow keeps pestering the rather unpleasant judge for justice against her enemy, and after first refusing her requests, the judge eventually gives her what she wants, in order to get a quiet life.

Some people have interpreted this to mean that we must continually bombard God with requests, and if we 'annoy' him enough then we might 'twist his arm' and convince him to grant our wishes (in order to shut us up). It's as if we think we can change God's mind - God will not answer my prayers if I ask him 100 times, but maybe if I ask 200 times then he will. It's an odd view of a loving God – detached and rather reluctant, he tallies up our requests until some magic number is reached, and then when he is heartily sick of our pleading, we get what we've asked for.

We pray about things not because we are telling God something he doesn't already know or care about, but because of our need to be connected to him, our wish to focus on something outside of ourselves. Prayer doesn't change God, but it can change us. Real prayer happens when I switch my focus away from *me* and what I want and need, so that my mind empties and my heart and soul are filled. In these moments we cease to be alone, recognising that we are sons and daughters of God, a part of God, or as St Paul put it 'hidden with Christ in God' (Colossians 3:3-4).

The key word in the parable is justice. The widow wanted justice and would not rest until she got it. Charities like CAFOD and Christian Aid campaign incessantly for an end to world poverty, not only raising money for those in need but continually bombarding politicians and decision makers with letters and petitions, and organising demonstrations and days of action. Their supporters never give up, determined to get a fair deal for the world's poor. The world is crying out for justice; there is much to pray about, and much to do, and we should never give up.

What I think Jesus is saying in the parable is that if the selfish and unpleasant judge can be persuaded to act justly then how much more readily will our loving God take care of our needs. Prayer is a conversation, we pause our busy lives and orient our gaze towards him, we connect with the divine. And together we consider the needs of the world or the pain of our sick friend. When we tell a friend they are 'in our prayers' we are not saying 'I have a special pathway to God and he will listen to my prayers for you and grant my request because I nag him'. We are saying 'I am thinking of you, God loves you and is close to you, you are in his hands - and I'm here to help whenever you need me'. This not only deepens our friendship with, and reliance on God, but also strengthens our connection with the person we are praying for.

In the words of Pope Francis, 'You pray for the hungry. Then you feed them. That's how prayer works.'

....

What part can I play in standing up for those who need help, for those who need justice?

99
—
We are all one

'May they all be one. Father, may they be one in us, as you are in me and I am in you, so that the world may believe it was you who sent me.'
(JOHN 17:21)

I was once told by a Christian clergyman that I shouldn't pray with people who belonged to other faiths - this would apparently displease Jesus. On another occasion one of my students informed me that although he had nothing against me personally (in fact we had a very friendly relationship), I would go to Hell for eternity because of my Christian beliefs. In his eyes it didn't matter that I was trying my best to be a good person - a belief that Jesus was the Son of God was enough to condemn me.

Such verbal disagreements are of course as nothing compared to the pain, misery and death caused by religious beliefs throughout human history. Within Christianity itself people have been tortured and burnt at the stake because they believed something slightly differently from their Christian brothers and sisters, for example a different belief about what happens at the Eucharist. Until the Second Vatican Council the Catholic Church proclaimed a rather harsh interpretation of the phrase, 'no salvation outside the Church'; in other words if you weren't a Catholic then you were in big trouble. Denominational and inter-faith relations are often merely a competition to prove who's right and who's wrong instead of an attempt to find common fellowship in the God who sees us all as his children.

In this extract from the Last Supper Jesus spells everything out in one sentence - the Father and Jesus are one, you are in God, and God is in you. Everyone is unique and individual, but we are all connected - to God and to one another, hence we all deserve to be loved and cared for. No-one is outside the tent, no-one is unlovable, no-one is excluded for any reason. If we fail to accept and include those who are different from us, those in other religions or races, those who are disadvantaged or in pain, then we haven't really listened to the prayer of Jesus – 'May they all be one'.

Today violence, religious and ethnic cleansing, and imprisonment due to religious beliefs are commonplace in much of the world, most recently the genocide of the Muslim Rohingya in Myanmar, and the forced detention of almost one million Muslims from the Uighur population in China. Three thousand Christians are put to death each year because of their faith. Yet when we look at the life of Jesus we see nothing but tolerance, understanding and the promotion of peace. How can a person believe that we are all brothers and sisters, and then condemn another for worshipping in a different building, or praying in a different way? It is not Jesus' way. For Jesus we are all part of the one body, and faith in him moves us from I to We.

Years ago, when I was a student, I used to help out in a homeless men's night shelter. It was run by an elderly Christian called Cyril. He was a Methodist I think, but he never discussed which particular church he worshipped in.

A number of local Christians of all denominations would volunteer to help out, and religion was often a topic of discussion. Cyril's contribution to these conversations was always very simple and direct - 'We are all one', he would say, and that phrase has stuck with me all my life. Unity between Christians and those of other faiths has come a long way in recent years, but there is still much work to be done. And praying together is a good way to begin.

....

Can I recognise my connection in Christ to everything and everyone?

100

—

Why Church?

'For where two or three meet in my name, I
shall be there with them.'
(Matthew 18:20)

During the covid-19 pandemic most of our churches were closed, and some people wondered whether they would ever go back to regular Sunday worship. They had got used to staying at home, sometimes just spending time in prayer or perhaps watching a service online. In the old days, in the Catholic church, it was a very serious sin to miss mass deliberately. I remember as a child when we went off for a week's holiday, the first thing my parents would do would be to find out where the nearest Catholic church was, and the Sunday Mass time. Of course our understanding of faith is different now, and we realise how ridiculous it was to suggest that your soul might be 'lost forever' if you decide not to attend Sunday worship.

However, there is something important about meeting together to pray once a week. It's not impossible to be a Christian on your own, but Christianity means community; we need others to minister to us, and we need, in turn, to minister to them. We are members of the body of Christ, links in a chain, each with our part to play. As part of a community we find opportunities to serve, to encourage, to provide a shoulder to lean on, and to pray for one another. It's a chance to use the gifts we have been given in the service of others. It is also a time to listen and learn, to try to hear what God might be telling us through his word and through the conversations we might have with others. From the early church onwards, Christianity has been about community and belonging and friendship; we journey together, not alone.

Sometimes we might get very little from going to church, but just showing up every week is a reminder to ourselves and to the community that this is an important priority in my life. We often hear the phrase 'I don't get anything out of going to church anymore', but perhaps we need to see that it's more about *giving* than getting.

Following Jesus is a communal activity; it's not primarily about me acquiring private salvation for myself as an individual whilst ignoring the rest of society. We are all in this together, no person is an island, we stand or fall with our brothers and sisters; we 'give life' to ourselves by helping to give life to others. One thing which covid-19 has perhaps taught us, is that we rely on each other, we depend on one another - our community, our common humanity, is crucial.

And of course in the Eucharist we give ourselves anew to God, and have the opportunity not just to be part of the body of Christ in community, but to receive Jesus into our hearts once more as we participate again in the meal of the Last Supper. Like the apostles we break bread together and renew our discipleship with the rest of our brothers and sisters. We acknowledge together our need of the saving love of Christ. Whether we are a 'regular' or a visitor on holiday, we come together, friend and stranger, united by our common faith that the incarnate God has come to live amongst us.

But there is little point going to church every Sunday if you don't practice the gospel for the rest of the week. As Pope Francis said, 'If I say I am Catholic and go to mass, but then don't speak with my parents, help my grandparents or the poor, go and see those who are sick, this does not prove my faith, there's no point'. He describes such people as 'Christian parrots' who only have 'words, words, words', and don't live out the gospel in their daily lives. Pope Francis concludes: 'Christian faith is expressed with three things: words, the heart and the hands'.

If I've stopped going to church, is it time for me to begin again?

101
—
Good luck? Bad luck?

Trust in the Lord with all your heart, and do not lean on your own understanding. In all your ways acknowledge him, and he will make straight your paths.
(Proverbs 3:5-6)

Anthony de Mello in his book 'Sadhana' re-tells an old Chinese story about a farmer whose only horse ran off into the hills. When his neighbours heard about his bad luck the farmer just said, 'Bad luck? Good luck? Who knows?' A week later the horse returned with a herd of wild horses from the hills and this time the neighbours congratulated the farmer on his amazing good fortune. His reply was, 'Good luck? Bad luck? Who knows?' Later that same day the farmer's son, whilst attempting to tame one of the wild horses, fell off and broke his leg. 'How unlucky' said the neighbours, but the farmer simply said, 'Bad luck? Good luck? Who knows?' Two weeks later the army arrived in the village and conscripted all the young men to fight in the war. However, the farmer's son was excused duty because of his broken leg. Was this good luck? Who knows?

During the Covid-19 lockdown when the dentists were closed, I suffered terrible toothache and reached for my rarely used rosary beads - the prayers I always say when pain or misfortune strikes and I don't have the strength to do anything else.

Nothing inspires us to pray like a crisis or fear or just plain 'bad luck'. I know people who don't believe in God who pray fervently when disaster strikes. When I asked my students if they prayed, many of them would say 'yes, the night before an important exam.'

All of us experience times of misfortune, sickness, worry, grief, pain and eventually the awareness that death is close at hand. We can feel hopeless and helpless, sometimes beside ourselves with anxiety. At such moments all we can do in prayer is trust. Trust in the loving mercy and wisdom of Christ who specifically asked us to come to Him and lay our burdens at his feet.

It is enough to trust that 'he will make straight your path'. We don't need to know exactly what lies ahead of us; we love to plan, to be in control, to map out the future, but Jesus just says 'Follow me'. We pray for answers, but Christ just wants trust, and a day-to-day dependence on him. This surrendering promotes humility and hope, giving us strength rather than making us powerless.

But there is a price to pay for trusting God and placing our worries in his hands - we must accept that the outcome may not be the one that we had wished for or prayed for. Trust means acceptance - that God loves us and *always* wants what is best for us, and will always look after us, 'yes, till the end of time'. It couldn't be any other way.

St Francis de Sales puts it like this, 'Do not fear what may happen tomorrow. The same loving Father who cares for you today will care for you tomorrow and every day. Either He will shield you from suffering, or He will give you unfailing strength to bear it. Be at peace, then, and put aside all anxious thoughts and imaginings'.

And when it comes to deciding what is good luck or bad luck it is best to leave that in God's hands – and be grateful that all things turn out for good with those who love him (Romans 8:28). In the words of Mother Julian of Norwich, the 14th century English mystic: 'All shall be well, and all shall be well, and all manner of things shall be well.'

....

Have the faith today to say, 'All shall be well'.

102

—

Loving God

Jesus said, 'You must love the Lord your God with all your heart, with all your soul, and with all your mind. This is the greatest and the first commandment. The second resembles it: You must love your neighbour as yourself.'
(MATTHEW 22:37-40)

Jesus tells us we are supposed to love God with all our heart and soul and to love our neighbour as ourself. At the Last Supper he calls his disciples *friends* rather than *servants*; rather than being served he wants to love and be loved. But how do we go about 'loving God'? It's not something we can just do, like turning on a tap, or saying 'OK from now on I will make sure I do this'. For some of us, loving our neighbour is possible (depending on the neighbour), but for many loving God is just not something they find feasible or realistic.

Where can we begin? According to many of the Church Fathers, a good place to start, perhaps the only place to start, is Creation, the natural world that God has fashioned. Pick up a pebble and admire its shape, colour and smoothness. Look at a flower or tree and see its complexity, grace and beauty - understand what it is adding to the world and its contribution to your joy and sense of wellbeing. Contemplate a bird outside or a pet perhaps, and appreciate the role it plays in your existence. Then move to other people, with all their faults and failings yes, but brothers and sisters, all with the Christ light within. In fact all of creation is suffused with the light of Christ which John reminds us was there at the very start of everything: 'In the beginning was the Word... All that came to be had life in him, and that life was the light of men'.

So try seeing the light of Christ in the created world, fall in love with the goodness and beauty all around you. Start small and move on up the chain. Try loving what's in front of you and see where this takes you. *We love God by loving what's there in the here and now: where else would God be found?* You can either live life just seeing God in certain holy places or specific 'easy to love' people, or you can see him everywhere. The way to love God is to love what he has created (everything) and those in whom he resides (everyone).

At first you might just catch small glimpses of God, but keep looking and listening and over time you will see more. Unlike turning on the tap this isn't a one-off event – it's a lifelong journey of discovery, an opening up, a new way of seeing, loving and praying.

Try loving what's in front of you today and see where this takes you.

STEP EIGHT

A New Way of Receiving

S ome theologians have talked about 'grit your teeth Christianity', a constant battle to be a better person, a better follower of Christ. However, rather than struggling to *achieve* (and then beating ourselves up when we fail) we often simply need to calmly open ourselves up to *receive*. In Step 8 Jesus shows us how to freely accept what God gives to us - the gifts of the Spirit and a Love which is eternal. When we hear Jesus telling us about the gifts he wants to give us, it all sounds just too good to believe – so we don't. But such gifts and opportunities are all around us; in the words of Paula D'Arcy, 'God comes to us disguised as our life'.

And of course we must also be open to learning and receiving wisdom and compassion from all of God's children including those of other faiths and none.

103
—
The Woman at the Well

*'Whoever drinks this water will get thirsty
again; but anyone who drinks the water that
I shall give will never be thirsty again: the
water that I shall give will turn into a spring
inside him, welling up to eternal life'.*
(JOHN 4:13-14)

We take water for granted - we turn on the tap and it's there. However according to UNICEF one in three people globally do not have access to safe drinking water.

In Jesus' time it was the women who drew water from the well, usually in the morning, to avoid the hottest part of the day. The unnamed Samaritan woman in this encounter with Jesus is there at midday, so is undoubtedly something of a social outcast. A Jewish man would not normally converse with a Samaritan woman, so Jesus is deliberately dismissing the predominant sexist and racist views of his day by having a long, frank conversation with her. She is surprised and wary when he asks her for a drink. When Jesus mentions that he is the source of 'living water', she replies with what might be interpreted as sarcasm. She almost says, who do you think you are? 'Are you a greater man than our father Jacob?' she asks. When

Jesus explains further, she is keen to accept what he is offering, especially when he tells her that she has had five husbands, and the man she is currently with is not her husband (she was later to tell the townsfolk: 'He told me all I had ever done'). The woman has heard about the Messiah, the Christ, and Jesus tells her, 'I who am speaking to you, I am he.'

Jesus just sees the woman as someone in need of help - who she is, her gender, marital status and ethnic background are irrelevant. He transforms her life. Jesus sees her, *notices* her, he affirms her value and worth even though she couldn't see it herself. The woman leaves her water jar where it is and hurries back to the town, and her testimony convinces many more to follow Jesus. The Gospel, rejected by the powerful scribes and elders, is embraced by the disregarded Samaritans, in fact John tells us that the townsfolk persuade him to stay on for two days to speak with them further. As for the woman, everyone wants to hear her story; redeemed by Jesus and outcast no more, perhaps she was even able to join the other women at the well in the early morning?

When you turn on your tap today you will get lots of fresh water to quench your thirst for a while. If you want living water, then you will have to turn elsewhere.

....

Pour yourself a glass of water today, and as you drink it, ask God for 'living water' - water that 'will turn into a spring inside you'.

104

—

Yes!

'I am the handmaid of the Lord' said Mary
'let what you have said be done to me.'
(LUKE 1:37-38)

Surveys have shown that most people are conservative by nature. We tend to be risk averse, and often say no to ventures if we are not certain of the outcome. Saying no to life's adventures rather than yes can mean that we close ourselves off to potential opportunity, change and growth. We don't like change, especially if it involves changing ourselves - we don't like the feeling of losing control over our environment. Change is often associated with uncertainty - like walking off a cliff blindfolded. Hence the phrase 'better the devil you know than the devil you don't know'. Sometimes we say no, rather than yes, because we are not sure if we have the ability or character to do what has been asked of us. Or perhaps we remember times past when we have taken a risk and it all 'ended in tears'.

When the angel appeared to Mary with God's plan for her future she had a choice to make, and the incarnation of Jesus was dependent on her decision. Luke says that 'she was deeply disturbed' by the words of the angel and her first thought must have been, 'No! Not me, I'm not ready for this, it's too risky.'

Whilst the angel waited for a response Mary asked questions, 'How can this come about?' Finally, Mary said yes, I will do it! She jumps off the cliff, risking an uncertain future with all the love and pain that will bring, because she trusts God.

Her leap of faith, her yes, brings Jesus into the world, and her life, and the lives of all of us will never be the same again. Her 'yes' ushers in great joy (and suffering too, that leads her eventually to the foot of the cross).

Just as at the Annunciation, God comes to us with the same request - he invites each of us to make Christ present in the world. Mary's 'yes' encourages us to say yes to Jesus, to bring him to birth in our lives too, and to accept the joy and pain that lie in store for each of us. Mary has been there before us and shown us the way.

Before we ever search for God, he is seeking us - he starts the conversation, and waits for our yes.

When we give up control and trust God we find a new freedom and a new type of control. When we can say with Mary 'thy will be done', then we let God be God, we allow grace to enter our life and change us. By losing control we gain control.

What is my response to God's invitation?

105

—

The gift of peace

*'Peace I give you, a peace the world cannot
give, this is my gift to you.'*
(John 14:27)

Advertisers love to sell us a dream - a dab of perfume or aftershave and you will become super-confident, poised and irresistible! So we end up spending an exorbitant amount on what is essentially coloured, smelly water, perhaps giving it as a gift for a friend on a special occasion.

During the Last Supper when Jesus knows he will soon have to leave the disciples he gives them a different kind of gift – 'my peace I give you, this is my gift to you.' Jesus knows how much we tend to worry and get anxious – he often tells his disciples that worrying is pointless and that 'tomorrow will take care of itself.' After gifting them his peace he says: 'Do not let your hearts be troubled or afraid'. It is an instruction, a command – stop worrying, trust in God, he is in control, all will be well. Jesus says, 'in this world you will have trouble', it is something we cannot avoid. However, peace is not an absence of trouble or conflict; it is the ability to cope with it.

Peace is not a passive activity; we must choose it and work at it. In 'The Imitation of Christ', Thomas à Kempis says,

'All men desire peace, but very few desire those things that make for peace.' We begin with ourselves; peace, like most things, begins at home. Forget the perfume or aftershave today. Instead ask God to clothe you with the spirit of peace, a peace of mind that is beyond all understanding and which allows us to cope with whatever life throws at us. Nothing should disturb our trust in his promise that 'all will be well', in God's good time. Our small decision to choose peace can flow from ourselves to our family and friends, and to our communities and nations. Peace is real and it's free; and like all good gifts it grows when it is shared.

....

What worries do I need to let go of, in order to accept Christ's gift of peace? How can I be a peacemaker in my family and community?

106

—

The Holy Spirit

'I shall ask the Father, and he will give you another Advocate to be with you for ever, the Spirit of truth.'
(JOHN 14:16)

The air we breathe is everywhere. You can't see it or touch it but it sustains your life with every breath you take. When the disciples were gathered in the upper room at Pentecost they had no idea that this air was about to become 'a powerful wind from heaven, the noise of which filled the entire house in which they were sitting ... They were all filled with the Holy Spirit' (Acts 2). This powerful wind from heaven turned their lives upside down; the fearfulness and doubt that had set in after Jesus' ascension disappeared in an instant, and from that moment on they had the strength and confidence to preach the gospel to all nations. The Christian Church as we know it was born - Pentecost Day became the Church's birthday.

Prior to this at the Last Supper, Jesus spoke his words of farewell to his disciples. If you have never read these words in their entirety, and you have a New Testament, it is worth putting this book down now, and doing so. They are some of the most beautiful words that have ever been written. Start at John 13:33 and continue to the end of John 17.

Jesus promises his disciples, and us, an 'Advocate', a word which comes from the Greek 'parakletos', and means 'one called alongside', a counsellor or protector. With the Father and Son, the Spirit is the third person of the Trinity. We see the Spirit at work in the opening verses of the Bible - the Spirit of God was 'hovering over the waters' (Genesis 1:12). Through the Old Testament prophets, God promises to 'pour out my spirit on all people' (Joel 2:28). When Mary was visited by an angel and consented to bear the child Jesus, she was told 'The Holy Spirit will come upon you' (Luke 1:35). Jesus in his ministry is 'led by the Spirit in the desert', and after he has read the lesson from Isaiah in the synagogue he says, 'The spirit of the Lord is on me.'

At the Last Supper Jesus promises his disciples that this Holy Spirit will lead them 'to the complete truth.' He 'will teach you everything and remind you of all I have said to you.'

St Paul tells us that the Spirit is a gift to us from God and 'the fruit of the spirit is love, joy, peace, patience, kindness, goodness, faithfulness, gentleness and self-control' (Galatians 5:22). The greatest of these is love.

Like the air we breathe that same Spirit is everywhere, unseen until the wind blows, but ever present and available to all without fear or favour. Jesus' promise to the disciples was a promise that we were meant to hear too. The Spirit isn't rationed, it's a free gift and not a reward for good behaviour. The only barrier to receiving the Spirit is our failure to ask for it - to trust, surrender and accept. The Spirit is not forced upon us - it's a gift freely given to those who ask. It's as simple as breathing.

Take a deep breath today and ask ... and you shall receive.

DOING CHRISTIANITY

107

—

Christmas gifts

There is a variety of gifts but always the same Spirit; there are all sorts of service to be done, but always to the same Lord; working in all sorts of different ways in different people, it is the same God who is working in all of them.
(1 Corinthians 12:4-7)

There is a store close to my house which puts on a lovely window display each Christmas. At the centre is a Christmas tree with dazzling baubles and fairy lights. Underneath are various presents, large and small, with beautiful wrapping paper and brightly coloured bows. I remember being impressed the first time I saw it, but the following year the same window display was put on show. The brightly coloured presents were there, exactly the same as before. The same unopened presents appeared each year, and as the years rolled by there was something sad about the scene - the presents that would never be opened, would never give delight to the recipient, would never trigger the love and gratitude that often comes from opening a gift at Christmas. I knew of course that they were just empty boxes for decoration; nevertheless they became a metaphor - for missed opportunities, life chances not taken, things left for another time, another year - gifts that always remained at the bottom of the tree, destined never to be received.

For some of us the gifts that God offers remain as unopened presents in our lives. Each year God offers us gifts of glad tidings, comfort, joy and peace to all people of goodwill - presents that last a lifetime and beyond. And unlike most earthly presents, once received they are designed to be passed on and given away to others - we are called to be living gifts to those around us.

Yet often we are reluctant to open these eternal gifts, offered to all, at no cost. It brings to mind a student who once said to me, 'I will think about God and what he has to offer when I'm older; I haven't got time for this religious stuff now, I'm young and I've got a life to lead!'

Each year God presents his gifts to us at the bottom of the Christmas tree, but he never forces us to receive them. He hopes that one day we *will* see them, open them enthusiastically, and be filled with gratitude for the 'pearl of great price' which is given to us. Unlike that pair of socks or new jumper which one day will wear out and turn to dust, this gift of himself will change our life and become something we will treasure forever.

....

Can I make a decision to become a living gift to those around me - not just at Christmas but throughout the year? Can I pass on the gift of God's love to those I meet today?

108

—

The Eucharist

Then he took some bread, and when he had
given thanks, broke it and gave it to them,
saying, 'This is my body which will be given
for you; do this as a memorial of me'.
(LUKE 22:19-20)

The word eucharist comes from the Greek and means thanksgiving. Celebrated at services throughout the Christian church, we remember and give thanks for the Last Supper, when Jesus broke bread with his disciples and asked them to 'do this in memory of me'. Jesus' presence in the bread and wine which becomes his body and blood is a complete mystery and is beyond our human understanding. In the end this does not matter - we are not called to fully understand the Eucharist but to live it, to experience it.

During the Catholic Eucharist the priest pours a tiny drop of water into the chalice of wine and quietly says the following prayer: 'By the mystery of this water and wine may we come to share in the divinity of Christ who humbled himself to share in our humanity'. It is a beautiful prayer: the drop of water symbolises our humanity and the wine will become the blood of Christ. Unlike say, water and oil, once blended together water and wine cannot be separated - the human and the divine become one.

St. Athanasius said, 'God became man, so that man might become like God'. If he had lived in the 21st century he might well have said, 'you are what you eat!' Person and God are inseparable - we share in his divine life. When we receive the Eucharist, we enter into union with God, our nature communes with the divine - in Holy Communion.

When we give God our humanity, he gives us his Divinity.

Pope Francis put it like this, 'Incarnation means that every person has been taken up into the very heart of God... conferring on them an infinite divinity.' God became man in Jesus so as to reveal to humanity the spark of divinity that dwells in all of us. After all, we are, all of us, made in the image and likeness of God. The Incarnation, God becoming man, the mixing of wine and water so that two become one, enabled St. Paul to say: 'you belong to Christ and Christ belongs to you.'

God feeds us, people of flesh and blood, by giving us his flesh and blood. The incarnation is made real and visible, we hold Christ in our hands for an instant and then we 'Take this and eat it'. Unlike the bread we consume in our daily lives Jesus describes himself as the 'living bread', the bread 'come down from heaven', which will satisfy our spiritual hunger. The Eucharist is an extraordinary event in many ways and demonstrates the intimacy Christ desires for our relationship with him. It is not to be a relationship of distance - he becomes a part of us, and we become a part of him.

Some of us may feel we cannot receive the Eucharist for one reason or another, perhaps because we feel we are sinful or unworthy. Sadly, some denominations restrict the Eucharist to those who are baptised or members of their particular church – those outside are considered to be 'not in communion', so cannot receive Communion. Yet the gospel shows us that Jesus is unconcerned with such strictures, happily breaking bread with prostitutes and 'sinners' of all description.

Pope Francis has said: 'sins do not define us', the Lord 'comes to heal them with the Eucharist'. That is why we say the words 'Lord I am not worthy to receive you' immediately before communion. The Eucharist is not a gift for the good, but a healing presence for the sinful. It is not a reward for holy members of an elite club but nourishment for the hungry. It is food for sinners not the virtuous.

However, there is work to do before we receive him. If we harbour anger, bitterness or ill-will towards others in our hearts then we need to make room for Jesus by gently releasing these feelings. There can be no room for Christ if we are full of our own pride and self-importance. At the Eucharist the bread and wine changes into the body and blood of Christ. But just as important is the change that needs to take place in us, the inner transformation that Christ wants and needs from us, changing our 'hearts of stone into hearts of flesh'. In the words of St John Chrysostom, 'If you do not find Christ in the beggar at the church door neither will you find him in the Chalice.'

If we fail to see and experience God in the everyday moments of our life then we will struggle to see and experience him in the Eucharist. But if we can see Christ in the bread and the wine then perhaps we can begin to see Christ in everything and everyone.

Inviting him in is a serious commitment. It demands some hard work and positive action. Finding room for Jesus in our lives means letting go of unhelpful ways of thinking and acting.

The priest consecrates the bread and wine, but once we receive Christ we are then commanded to go forth and likewise consecrate all we do and all we meet. The way we experience the love and mercy of God is through each other. We too are commissioned to bless and encourage, to heal and forgive, to bring the divine presence to others. This is what is meant by the final words of Sunday worship: 'Go in peace to love and serve the Lord.'

....

Do I make time in my life to receive the 'living bread?'

109

—

It's a Mystery

'but the Advocate, the Holy Spirit, whom
the Father will send in my name, will
teach you everything and remind you of
all I have said to you.'
(JOHN 14:26)

In the Great Schism of 1054 the Western and Eastern churches split apart. Why was this? Did they disagree on something important such as the primacy of loving kindness or the role of forgiveness and compassion in the Christian life? No. The split concerned theological belief, namely does the Holy Spirit proceed from the Father and the Son, or from the Father alone? Heaven knows why they thought this was important enough to divide the Christian church in two but it did, with the Patriarch of Constantinople and the envoys of Pope St Leo IX excommunicating each other!

During my childhood RE lessons at school if anyone asked a difficult question about faith, and the teacher couldn't think of an answer, they would usually say 'it's a mystery'. We all knew this meant they probably didn't know! Maybe we all need to say 'I don't know' more often when talking about religion - a phrase that might have been useful in 1054. There is no such thing as absolute certainty. Not knowing everything keeps us humble and questioning, two good traits.

The Trinity is undoubtedly a 'mystery' - three persons in one God (Father, Son and Spirit). I remember a teacher trying to explain it using the analogy of water, steam and ice, and I vividly remember one pupil describing it as a hamburger - meat, bun and relish - which I guess wouldn't have gone down all that well with Leo IX and the Patriarch!

A better explanation of the Trinity came from the early Church Fathers who used the Greek word 'perichoresis', which some scholars have defined as a 'circle dance'. It describes a continuous, intimate fellowship between the three persons. St Bernard of Clairvaux explained this by saying, 'If...the Father is he who kisses, the Son he who is kissed, then it cannot be wrong to see in the kiss the Holy Spirit... their unshakable bond, their undivided love, their indivisible unity.' There is a perfect loving communion at work here; Trinity is about each connecting to the other in perfect relationship. We can see this in the first three lines of Genesis 1: Father God, the light of Christ and the Spirit 'hovering' over the water, all engaged in the wonder of creation.

The sterile theological debates of 1054 should not stop us from *participating* in what Richard Rohr describes as the Trinitarian 'divine dance'. We are not to stand alone, God has made room for us on the dance floor, and we are called to experience the love that resides there. Yes, the Trinity is a mystery, but it's one we can partake in, which is what St Paul meant when he said: 'The grace of the Lord Jesus Christ, the love of God and the fellowship of the Holy Spirit be with you all' (2 Corinthians 13:13).

....

Am I ready to join in 'the divine dance'?

110

—

Learning from others

'God does not see as man sees; man looks at
appearances but Yahweh looks at the heart.'
(1 SAMUEL 16:7)

I once read in the paper about a yoga teacher who was barred
by the vicar from using an Anglican church hall in England
for her classes because such activities were deemed to be
incompatible with the Christian faith. The objection seemed
to be that because yoga has connections with both Hinduism
and Buddhism then it had no place being practised in a church
hall. There was a suggestion that Pilates might be more suit-
able (no relation to Pontius!). I thought this might be a one-
off, but later discovered that yoga classes were banned in some
halls in Australia after a Church report found that it might lead
Christians to 'worshipping false gods'.

Christians can sometimes think they have a monopoly on truth, and Muslims, Hindus, Jews, Sikhs, Buddhists, or
Humanists have nothing to teach us. The risk with seeing ourselves as a kind of 'chosen people' is that everyone else becomes those who haven't been chosen! God loves and cares
for us, but no-one else! Jesus warned against travelling down
this path when he said that not everyone who says, 'Lord,
Lord' is to be trusted, and those who don't profess 'Lord Lord'

may yet be doing 'the will of my Father in heaven'. Many of us have forgotten that Jesus was a Jew (Christianity came later).

If we believe that Christ dwells in all, then all have the potential for goodness and wisdom - anyone can reflect the Christ light to others. Many Humanists, for example, work tirelessly to promote social justice, and their belief in the importance of spreading love, respect and compassion to all of humanity is a philosophy that most religions share. So often we are quick to judge and condemn, wanting everything to be done our way or not at all. This way of thinking excludes rather than includes - the very opposite of the message Jesus came to bring.

We highlight the divisions between us, but these divisions are generally doctrinal and irrelevant, akin to medieval theologians debating how many angels can fit on a pinhead. Sometimes we become obsessed with how we worship: 'you must pray this way, you must say these words, in these places, at these times'. Jesus put the Pharisees in their place by quoting the prophet Hosea, 'Go and learn the meaning of the words: *What I want is mercy, not sacrifice*' (Matthew 9:13). Jesus always focuses on what really matters - how we relate to each other and to God on a day-to-day basis.

For some strange reason we want God to be 'ours', we see ourselves in competition with other faiths, we find it hard to accept that God is in other religions, or in those with no faith. Listen to St. Paul's startling words as he preaches the gospel to the non-Christian Athenians in Acts 17:23: 'the God whom I proclaim is in fact the one you already worship without knowing it'. He goes on to say, 'he is not far from any of us, since it is in him that we live, and move, and exist ... we are all his children'.

We are created in the image and likeness of God, but each cultural and historical group tends to create God in *their* own image and likeness: 'God is ours, not yours, he is with us not you!' We are most comfortable with a God like us - anything unfamiliar is often perceived as a threat and a challenge.

The reality is that God is either everywhere or nowhere. We can't put him in a little tabernacle just for 'the faithful'. He isn't that small or petty. He belongs to everyone, and he is everywhere.

I will leave the last word to the Reverend Deborah Parsons, a Church of England Interfaith Advisor who, when asked to comment on the yoga ban in her diocese said: 'We're invited to be curious, to listen to difference and to re-imagine how to be Love's Presence in every community. Through respectful listening we can come to a deeper understanding of each other. Jesus the Christ modelled this by his engagement with and love for the outsider. He crossed borders and boundaries and questioned taboos. He spread an aroma of love.'

What can I learn from other faith traditions and ways of thinking?

111

—

In the same boat as Paul

Christy is in you...
(Romans 8:10-11)

Jesus was a Jew, the religion about him is Christianity.
St Paul is perhaps the single most important follower of
Christ when it comes to establishing this new religion. It
is interesting to note that Paul never knew Jesus and before
his conversion on the road to Damascus enthusiastically persecuted Christians.

Paul, someone who never knew *Jesus* of Nazareth, reveals
in his Letters what he knows about the *Christ*, who has always
existed from the beginning of time and who lives today in everything and everyone. Unlike the disciples this knowledge
was not acquired by listening in person to Jesus preach but
through the actions of the Holy Spirit, which began when he
was thrown from his horse near Damascus. In other words,
Paul is like us.

Paul's contribution is immense. He confirms the key message that Jesus gave the disciples at the Last Supper - Christ
lives in us: 'the love of God has been poured into our hearts by
the Holy Spirit which has been given to us' (Romans 5:5). In
2 Corinthians Paul asks us, 'Do you acknowledge that Jesus
Christ is really in you?' Imagine for a moment who we could

become if we allowed that acknowledgement to be our ever-present guiding principle. And what if we became aware that the Father is always seeing and loving the Christ who lives in us?

Interestingly, when we begin to live in Christ, we live no longer for ourselves, yet strangely, we are actually more ourselves than we have ever been.

Paul goes on to destroy all the tribal ways of thinking that bedevil society: 'there are no more distinctions between Jew and Greek, slave and free, male and female, but all of you are one in Christ Jesus' (Galatians 3:28).

Christ is in all, and for all. This is the oft-neglected cornerstone of our faith, the foundational reality on which the whole Gospel rests. Paul is in the same boat as us. He didn't know the historical Jesus, but he did know the risen Christ. This relationship with Christ is available to us too - what Paul experienced and preached can, through the actions of a generous God, be our lived experience too.

....

Imagine who we would become if we thought, spoke and acted with the belief that Christ lives in us. Can I acknowledge with Paul that 'Christ is really in me'?

STEP NINE

Coming Home

. . . .

Truly, Yahweh was always in this place all the time,
and I never knew it.
(JACOB WAKING UP FROM HIS SLEEP – GENESIS 28:16)

We shall not cease from exploration
And the end of all our exploring
Will be to arrive where we started
And know the place for the first time.
(T.S. ELIOT)

As we approach the end of our 'virtual pilgrimage' we might ponder the fact that 'the Christian life is more like following a path than it is about believing things with our minds' (Marcus Borg).

This book is called 'Doing Christianity', so in this Ninth Step we pull everything together and think about what we might need to be doing now. We are all at different stages on our journey, but wherever we are we can be sure that God is with us, loving us into new life with him and with all that he has created and urging us to 'make our home in him'.

112

—

Making our home in you

'I am in my Father and you in me and I in you
... If anyone loves me he will keep my word,
and my Father will love him, and we shall
come to him and make our home with him.'
(JOHN 14:20-23)

For most of us home is a lovely place. It is a refuge, somewhere we can relax, recharge our batteries and be ourselves. A house is just a roof over our head; a home is a place to come back to, a place of welcome and love. At the end of a busy day, it is a good feeling to 'make our way home'. Home is where the heart is.

Jesus understands what homelessness means. In Bethlehem there was no room for his family at the inn, and during the three years of his ministry he had no home: 'Foxes have holes and the birds of the air have nests, but the Son of Man has nowhere to lay his head'. At the Last Supper Jesus reveals to the disciples that he wants to make his home in their hearts.

He has already told his disciples that the Holy Spirit will be with them when he has gone, but he makes it clear in this verse that he is in the Father, and 'you in me and I in you'. This is a different kind of trinity - Father, Jesus and you. Every encounter with Jesus is also an invitation, and this one is difficult to refuse. If we are prepared to follow Jesus, to keep his 'word' by our actions and our love for one another, then God will make his home in us. He will reside with us, wherever we are, there *He* will be - our place of safety and welcome. And if God lives with us then there is nothing in life that we cannot face, no problem we cannot overcome together, no time when we can feel homeless or abandoned. If God has made his home in us then we are never alone.

....

Consider for a moment the possibility of God 'making his home with you'. Wherever you live and wherever you go, he will be there for you.

113

—

Come and have breakfast!

Simon Peter went aboard and dragged the net to the shore, full of big fish, one hundred and fifty three of them; and in spite of there being so many the net was not broken. Jesus said to them, 'Come and have breakfast'.

(JOHN 21:11-12)

When the disciples were with Jesus they would have been supported by the charity of others, but after the Resurrection they were forced to return to their previous occupation as fishermen. They go out onto the Sea of Galilee but catch nothing - John seems to be saying that without Jesus 'they can do nothing'. In fact the disciples never catch a fish in the whole of the gospel without the aid of Jesus!

A figure they don't recognise appears on the shore and tells them to drop their net into the water on the other side of the boat. Here they catch an enormous haul of fish, and looking up John realises that the man is the Risen Christ and cries out, 'It is the Lord'. When they come ashore they see that Jesus has prepared a charcoal fire and bread saying, 'Bring some of the fish you have just caught... Come and have breakfast'. John specifies that exactly 153 fish were caught. St. Jerome suggested that this was because there were 153 known species of fish in the world at this time; hence this is an indication that Jesus wants the disciples to become fishers of men in all nations.

Jesus prepares a meal for the disciples and they recognise him in the breaking of bread. It's always lovely when someone invites you for food and conversation. We too are invited to join him on the lakeside, we are always welcome at the table of the Lord. We may have got out of the habit of saying 'Grace before meals', but it is good to reflect on the fact that whenever we break bread together with family and friends, Christ is there. We are invited to see every dining table or picnic blanket as an altar, an opportunity for communion and fellowship.

After the meal Jesus asks Peter three times if he loves him. This echoes Peter's three denials of Jesus round another charcoal fire before his crucifixion. Each time Peter is asked, he professes his love for Jesus. This is Christ the healer; he gives the disciple who was the rock on which the early church would be built, an opportunity to repent, to acknowledge his previous lack of faith, and receive the life-giving forgiveness and reconciliation that only God can bring.

This episode is almost a summary of the whole gospel for Peter and for us. Jesus provides for us, we meet him in the breaking of bread, we acknowledge our brokenness and pride, and we repent and believe in the Good News. In short, we are healed and made whole by the love of God. Jesus then gives Peter, and us, the commission to 'feed my sheep'. After repentance comes self-awareness, and the command to help others, but always with the knowledge that Christ will be by our side in all our endeavours.

....

Spend some time today imagining yourself by the lakeside and hearing Christ say to you, 'Come and have breakfast'.

114

—

Free Trial

the two disciples followed Jesus. Jesus turned
round, saw them following and said, 'What
do you want?' They answered, 'Rabbi,' -
which means Teacher - 'where do you live?'
'Come and see' he replied...
(JOHN 1:37-39)

I saw an advertisement in a magazine for a pair of slippers. They promised to be the lightest, softest, comfiest pair of slippers you had ever worn. Moreover, the ad went on, 'try them for a month and if you are not completely satisfied then send them back for a full no-quibble refund'. It was a persuasive advert - they were clearly very confident of their product.

If you are not yet convinced that Jesus is someone worth following then I wonder if you might be interested in trying the Gospel for a month and seeing how you get on, knowing that of course you can always decide to 'hand it all back' later if you're not happy. This is what Jesus said to the disciples: 'Come and see', give it a go, try this for size - you have nothing to lose.

To begin with, try accepting that you are loved by God and that God lives in you. See how that goes for a while. See if you can place any anxieties you may have at the feet of Christ, one worry at a time. Don't think about it too much, in the words of Nike - 'Just do it!' Try looking at other people in a new way - see if you can spot the goodness in them, the spark of the divine in every person you meet. Can you experiment with generosity? Try becoming a bit more generous with your love, your care, your time and your money (if you are able, make a donation to a favourite charity). Have a go at spending five minutes each day just sitting and breathing, repeating a simple prayer such as 'Come, Lord Jesus', and try dipping into a page of John's Gospel every day and seeing what Christ might be saying to you.

Make a conscious effort when you wake up to try and do everything you can each day with a joyful heart and see how that feels - be present or mindful as much as you can; everything is gift, stay in the moment, imagine the presence of Christ and be grateful for whatever it is you are doing. If you have any anger or bitterness towards others in your heart try releasing all of that, and then ask Christ to replace it with trust, gratitude and above all love. Place love (for yourself and others) at the centre of all your daily interactions, the be-all and end-all of everything you do. See if that makes a difference to how you feel about yourself and others. Learn to appreciate that Christ is Love, and Love is everything: the reason we are here, our guide along the way, and the answer to all life's problems.

....

And don't forget the 'full no-quibble guarantee'. Once the free trial is over you can either 'hand back the Gospel' and return to your previous life, no questions asked, or continue the adventure.

115

—

The Home is a Church

Every house is built by someone, but God is
the builder of everything.
(HEBREWS 3:4-5)

Humans love to compartmentalise and tidy. In our kitchen we have drawers and cupboards set aside for all our cooking implements. Each has its proper home, and woe betide anyone if the cheese grater or tin opener is put back in the wrong place!

For many of us, our religion is compartmentalized. On Sunday we might go to church for an hour, recognising the importance of God in our lives, but for the rest of the week it's 'business as usual'. Faith becomes a leisure activity like our weekly game of tennis perhaps, or our regular coffee meet-up with friends. But what if we saw things differently? What if every day became a Sunday? What if our home became our church, our 'domestic church', a place where we showed God to each other by our forgiveness, love and selflessness? What if we became the priests (male and female of course) in this domestic church? Each hug becomes a sign of peace, each word of encouragement becomes a hymn of praise, each small act of self-sacrifice for our family becomes our offertory procession. Our 'I Confess' becomes a readiness to forgive and say sorry, and instead of listening to the homily, we listen patiently to our partner or child telling us about their day.

We become the gospel for each other. The Creed, the 'I Believe', becomes our opportunity to tell our family members how much we believe in them, trust them and hope in them. The dinner table becomes the Eucharistic table, where we make holy the bread and wine of all that happens in our family. By allowing Christ to 'enter under our roof', we consecrate our home to him; and by the loving conversations we have with one another we make real the communion prayer, 'only say the word and my soul shall be healed'.

There aren't two kinds of love or compassion - a divine one and a human one. There is only one. God loves us through each other. God forgives us through each other (see the Our Father). God blesses us through each other. In the past many theologians have wrongly separated God and man, the divine and the worldly, the holy and the profane. The incarnation of Jesus, where the human and the divine meet, shows us that there is no distinction, no dualism - God is everywhere and in everything, and it is through the ordinary events of our life that he loves us and saves us.

The Incarnation means that Christ cannot be tidied away and put in a box labelled 'Sunday worship'. My soul can be healed every day in the heart of my family. Every day is Christ's day, every home is a church, all is sacred.

....

And don't just stop with the home. Imagine if your workplace was a church...

DOING CHRISTIANITY

116

—

Eternal Life

'Jesus,' he said, 'remember me when
you come into your kingdom'. 'Indeed, I
promise you' he replied 'today you will be
with me in paradise.'
(Luke 23:42-43)

Imagine if the modern news media had been around when Jesus brought Lazarus back from the dead after four days in the tomb. Reporters would have been fighting for that first interview with Lazarus, and a bidding war would be breaking out amongst newspaper editors for 'the full and exclusive story'. The first question Lazarus would have been asked might have been, 'what was it like after you passed away?'

Benjamin Franklin told us that nothing is certain except death and taxes. We all know how much tax we pay, but what happens at our death? The short answer of course is that no-one really knows for sure. Various people have written about near death experiences (NDEs) when individuals have died medically and then been resuscitated. Many report having similar experiences such as: becoming detached from the physical body, feelings of unconditional love and peace, seeing a light and entering the light.

Some of these NDEs include being briefly reunited with loved ones who have already passed away. Several neuroscientists and psychologists have argued that such phenomena could also have a scientific explanation based on brain activity. However, what is not open to dispute is that the overwhelming majority of those who experience NDEs come back with a sense of peace, a greater appreciation of life, less concern for material goods, greater compassion for others and a heightened sense of spirituality. They also report no longer having a fear of death.

So without that interview with Lazarus, and knowing we will never be able to prove anything, we fall back on faith. Jesus' teaching is clear; the gospel writers record him making over a dozen references to 'eternal life.' Just before his death on the cross he promises the man who is being crucified next to him that he will be with him later that day in paradise. At the Last Supper Jesus tells his disciples: 'Do not let your hearts be troubled. Trust in God still, and trust in me. There are many rooms in my Father's house; if there were not, I should have told you. I am going now to prepare a place for you, and after I have gone and prepared you a place, I shall return to take you with me; so that where I am you may be too.'

It may surprise you to learn that most of the references to eternal life in the Gospels describe a feast, a banquet, a party, a wedding reception. There is only one description of judgement (Matthew 25:13-46), and here the focus is on how we need to look after the hungry, the thirsty, the stranger and the prisoner. The main message of Jesus is an open invitation to those out on 'the open roads and the hedgerows'. *Everyone* is invited to the feast if they want to come.

If Christ lives in us, then we also partake in his Resurrection - we are destined for eternal life. We often say 'love never dies', and we who share in 'the divine nature' (2 Peter 1:4), held in God's embrace, must also share in the promise of the resurrection.

....

Jesus asks his disciples, and us, to trust him - one day he shall return to take us to him. In the darkness of death Jesus will be our light, guiding us home. We are all invited to the party.

117

—

The Problem with 'Defending the Faith'

'Why do you observe the splinter in your brother's eye and never notice the plank in your own?'
(MATTHEW 7:3-4)

Hans Kung, author of the highly acclaimed 'On Being a Christian', is widely regarded as one of the most influential Catholic theologians of the twentieth century. He played an important role in the Second Vatican Council (1962-65) which resulted in a new openness in the Church and an historic dialogue with other Christians and those of other faiths. However, in 1979 the Sacred Congregation for the Doctrine of the Faith, a Vatican body tasked with ensuring doctrinal orthodoxy, declared that he had 'departed from the integral truth of Catholic faith, and therefore he can no longer be considered a Catholic theologian nor function as such in a teaching role.' Along with other things Kung disagreed with the Vatican's literal interpretation of the doctrine of papal infallibility. Kung was forced out of the Catholic faculty at his German university (though he continued to teach in the university's Institute for Ecumenical Research).

This decision reflects a mindset common in many Christian denominations (including some Evangelical churches in America), where the main purpose of organised religion can appear to be 'protecting the faithful from error'. The preoccupation here is on 'thinking the right things' and woe betide anyone who steps out of line. The organisation which represents most Catholic nuns in America has been consistently censured by the Vatican - in 2012 it was accused in a damning Vatican report, of promoting 'certain radical feminist themes incompatible with the Catholic faith.' One such incompatibility was the persistent questioning of whether the Church needs to retain an all-male priesthood.

Such a response is about keeping control, it's the church as 'thought police'; being 'right' and winning becomes more important than admitting there is ambiguity and uncertainty.

Things have changed a little in the papacy of Francis but there is still an element of defending the faith, like soldiers in a fortress, watching out for those who question and debate too much. Too often Christian churches have adopted an 'either-or' philosophy – you are either right or wrong, either with us or against us. This can result in a slavish devotion to old certainties, protecting the past at all costs rather than creating a future where people feel welcomed and included. Sometimes the need to 'keep faith with tradition' is invoked by those who yearn to keep things just as they have always been. However, Pope Francis pointed out after his 2022 visit to Canada that, 'Tradition is the living faith of the dead... not the dead faith of the living... Tradition is not a piece that belongs in a museum... A church that doesn't evolve is a church that goes backwards.'

Vatican II was successful because it accepted that 'to live is to change' (Newman) and this culture of renewal and openness is vital if the church is to win back the hearts of those who have drifted away and those young people who were never really engaged in the first place. Having, maintaining and enforcing a set of correct beliefs about God or the Church just doesn't work anymore. Not for US nuns, not for anyone.

Instead of embracing uncertainty and allowing healthy debate the Christian churches have often placed dogmatism before an honest acceptance that things are often more grey than black and white. The author of 'On Being a Christian' died in 2021 but I think he would agree that being a faithful Christian is not a search for certainty, but learning to place our trust in a God who loves us. It is more about being connected than being correct.

....

How can I become less fearful of uncertainty and change?

118

—

Abide in Me

*'I am the true vine, and my Father is the
vinedresser. Every branch in me that bears
no fruit he cuts away, and every branch that
does bear fruit he prunes to make it bear even
more... Make your home in me, as I make
mine in you... I am the vine, you are the
branches. Whoever remains in me, with me in
him, bears fruit in plenty; for cut off from me
you can do nothing.'*
(JOHN 15:1-5)

Have you ever counted up the number of places you
have ever called 'home'? For me, it is eleven. Most of
us tend to wander around a bit, especially when we
are younger, and our souls are often restless too, searching
for meaning, looking for a permanent home.

Jesus was a nomad for the last three years of his life, and
the wandering lifestyle would have been a familiar one to his
disciples too. Yet Jesus offers his followers a permanent spiritual home or 'abode'. 'Abide in me' he says, 'as I abide in
you'. It is The Last Supper, and Jesus is making the central
message of the Gospel crystal-clear to the apostles. I already

live in you, he says, and you must understand this, and abide in me too. The vine (Christ) and the branch (us) are one. The life of the vine flows into each branch, giving it shape and purpose. If any parts of the branch are not producing good fruit - perhaps they are only producing egotistical and selfish benefits (fruit that doesn't last) - then they can be pruned and cast aside. Jesus is saying, stay connected to me, and I will produce real 'fruit in plenty', fruit that will last. This life-blood transforms the branch into a thing of beauty, as well as helping each branch to entwine with neighbouring branches, providing strength and support to them when needed.

Wherever we call 'home' on this earth, wherever we are physically, in a mansion or a slum or a prison, then Christ is with us, and his life will flow through us. At the Last Supper Jesus initiates the Eucharist, asking the apostles to drink the fruit of the vine and work of human hands, the wine, his blood. It is a wonderful sign of Christ's ongoing life in us and our joint endeavour to provide the fruits of loving kindness and compassion to all.

What needs to be pruned in my life if I am to bear fruit in plenty?

119

—

Teflon Gospel?

Then they said to him, 'What must we do if
we are to do the works that God wants?'
(JOHN 6:28-29)

Ronald Reagan was known as the 'Teflon President' in the United States - he always seemed to avoid blame or responsibility for anything bad that happened. Nothing ever seemed to stick to him. Even the term 'Teflon President', which was designed as a criticism became something he was admired for!

What is our reaction when we hear Jesus in the Gospel telling us how to live our lives? What is our response for example when he says we must forgive someone 'seventy times seven' or 'turn the other cheek'? The most common reaction is for us to feel challenged, a bit uncomfortable perhaps, and then do nothing. It's as if it all skates over us, quickly sliding off our consciousness as if it were coated in teflon. Nothing sticks!

Why is this? Are we sceptical that Jesus actually said such things? Perhaps we think that not everything Jesus said is actually true, or perhaps his words have been misreported? Maybe we think he was speaking completely in metaphor, so he didn't *actually* mean forgiving everybody all the time? Perhaps we think that we *should* do it, but we *can't* - it's just too difficult? You might think that Jesus was setting us a very high bar, he was an idealist, a dreamer - in practical terms what he is asking us to do is impossible, and faintly ridiculous - the world isn't like that; maybe Jesus was exaggerating just to make a point? Some of us might feel it's true but consider ourselves too sinful, just not good enough or holy enough, so there's no point in even trying to follow Jesus' teaching. Perhaps we are afraid of failure, so we don't even try? Others may cynically feel that if we did forgive continually we would look foolish in the eyes of the world, we might be 'taken advantage of' or 'taken for a fool', seen as weak or soft by others - our self-esteem would take a hit. Maybe we just don't have the courage to go against the accepted wisdom of the age, too embarrassed to go against the crowd, or look foolish in front of our peers.

Our reluctance to actually put the gospel into practice is a reflection of how we see ourselves, how we see God and how we see other people. If we have a negative view of ourselves as weak or failing, if we see Jesus as a hard taskmaster or an impractical dreamer, if we view others with suspicion and fear rather than openness and love, then the words in the gospel will often slide off us and go nowhere.

But what if we trust God, trust that Christ loves us and has our best interests at heart? What if we believe that Christ never asks us to do anything which we are not capable of carrying out? What if we believe that the Holy Spirit will always give us the strength and power to do the right thing? And what if the world and everyone in it is graced and loved by God, what if Christ truly lives in my neighbour, and by forgiving another I am loving and accepting the Christ who resides within them? What if forgiving others is actually the road map to happiness and freedom. What if the gospel is *the truth*?

....

> *How do the views I have of myself, God and the world affect the way I respond to the Gospel?*

120

—

Terms and Conditions

'Come to me, all you who labour and are
overburdened, and I will give you rest.
Shoulder my yoke and learn from me, for I
am gentle and humble in heart, and you will
find rest for your souls. Yes, my yoke is easy
and my burden light.'
(Matthew 11:28-30)

Whenever you decide to agree to something on the internet you generally have to read and assent to a whole series of 'Terms and Conditions' - you can sometimes feel that you are signing your life away. When I taught in a sixth form college all new students had to agree to and sign the College Regulations before they could be enrolled. So what do I need to sign up to if I want to be a follower of Jesus?

Some churches may well have a list of 'terms and conditions' - things you need to believe in, or doctrines you need to agree to, before you can be 'admitted'. However, these do vary widely depending on the denomination.

As this book hopefully makes clear, the Gospel of Jesus is not so much about what you believe but how you act, how you trust and in particular how you love. What is essential if you wish to follow Christ is to believe in love, and it's trans-forming power. Without that, as St Paul says, we are nothing.

> *If I have all the eloquence of men or of angels, but*
> *speak without love, I am simply a gong booming*
> *or a cymbal clashing. If I have the gift of prophe-*
> *cy, understanding all the mysteries there are, and*
> *knowing everything, and if I have faith in all its*
> *fulness, to move mountains, but without love, then*
> *I am nothing at all. If I give away all that I possess,*
> *piece by piece, and if I even let them take my body to*
> *burn it, but am without love, it will do me no good*
> *whatever ... In short, there are three things that*
> *last: faith, hope and love; and the greatest of these is*
> *love. (1 Corinthians 13:1-13)*

That's it really - everything else then comes down to how this transformative power of love leads us to act in ways that leave our ego-centred self behind, so we can embrace our new life with Christ, seeing him in everyone and everything. And if we are trying to be a good person, then we are already reflecting the light of God within, whether we acknowledge that or not.

Jesus didn't leave behind a set of complicated terms and conditions to sign; on the contrary he tells us that he will not overburden us: 'my yoke is easy'. We're not signing our life away when we follow Christ - we are opening the door to 'living life to the full'.

....

Am I happy to 'sign up' for this 'life with Christ?'

121

—

Being a Christian is easy...

'with God all things are possible.'
(MATTHEW 19:26)

As we come to the end of our virtual pilgrimage it is worth reminding ourselves that if we were walking from London to Walsingham we would now have walked 120 miles and arrived at the Slipper Chapel, which is one mile from the Shrine in the centre of the village. The next step is both very easy and very difficult. Taking off your shoes at the Slipper Chapel is the easy bit, but walking the last 'Holy Mile' in bare feet is difficult and often painful! It's all a perfect metaphor for being a Christian.

Being a Christian is easy because Jesus tells us so: 'my yoke is easy and my burden is light'. He invites us to make our home in him, as he makes his home in us. His promise is that we shall have life and have it to the full. He will freely provide us with 'living water', and we will never be thirsty again. When we are in trouble and overburdened, he gives us rest and peace, a peace that passes all understanding. He freely shares his joy with us and tells us that with him 'all things are possible'. We are his brothers and sisters - and he calls us friends. If we come to him, he will never turn us away.

It's easy to say 'yes' to this love. It's easy to say 'fill me with your Spirit'; it's easy to say 'Lord Lord', and we don't have any problem saying, 'give us this day our daily bread, and forgive us our trespasses'. It's easy to 'ask and receive'. Most of us can accept with hope and gladness the promise of eternal life. Saying 'yes' to all this - why wouldn't you?

But 'doing' Christianity is more difficult. It's hard to love your neighbour as yourself, and forgive 'those who trespass against us'. When we are asked for our shirt, it's hard to also hand over our coat. Loving your enemies is one of the hardest things anyone can be asked to do. It's easy to drop a few coins into a charity collection box, it's not so easy to sell your 'treasured' possessions and give your money to the poor. It's hard to live out Jesus' instruction to not 'worry about your life, what you will eat or what you will drink' when there are bills dropping through the letterbox. It's much easier to follow the wide path, than enter by the narrow gate. It's hard 'to deny yourself', and particularly tough to rejoice when we are persecuted for doing the right thing.

In short, it's easy to believe in the teachings of Jesus, it's another thing to live them out in practice. It's not that difficult to turn up in church now and again or say the 'Our Father' once in a while, but this is to treat faith as a pastime like gardening or playing bridge. It's much harder to imitate Christ in all we do.

Putting all our trust in God and putting into practice the Gospel of Jesus, week in week out - that's the hard bit. That's taking up our cross and following him. The Gospel challenges us, it threatens our complacency; it shakes us up, but this is a crucial and necessary step. Before we can be inspired and lifted up, before we can be transformed, we must first be disturbed and made uncomfortable.

But we know that he is by our side every step of the way. Of course we will fall and fail repeatedly, and get lost, but Christ knows this, and like the Good Shepherd, he always comes back for us and brings us home.

....

This is God's promise. This is the 'good news' of the Gospel of Jesus Christ.

Your virtual pilgrimage has come to an end, but your journey continues.

Where will your next steps take you?